Books by Florence Page Jaques
Illustrated by Francis Lee Jaques

CANOE COUNTRY

THE GEESE FLY HIGH

BIRDS ACROSS THE SKY

SNOWSHOE COUNTRY
   (*Awarded 1946 John Burroughs Medal*)

CANADIAN SPRING

Canadian Spring

By Florence Page Jaques

Illustrations by Francis Lee Jaques

Harper & Brothers, Publishers, New York and London

10-7

Canadian Spring

Copyright, 1947, by Francis Lee Jaques
and Florence Page Jaques

Printed in the United States of America

All rights in this book are reserved. No part of the
book may be reproduced in any manner whatsoever
without written permission except in the case of brief
quotations embodied in critical articles and reviews.
For information address Harper & Brothers

First Edition

H-W

As they keep on telling me one cannot inscribe a book to one's fellow-collaborator, I will dedicate this fifth result of our joint endeavors

TO

LEE'S GREAT NORTH ROAD

Long may it run between the Bay of the Woolly Mammoths and the Millennium Mills.

Acknowledgments

I WISH to express our gratitude to H. Albert Hochbaum, who urged us to write this book, and who was untiring in showing us the Manitoba region, as were his colleagues, Peter Ward, Lyle Sowls, and their families. To Al Hochbaum I also owe the greatest debt for his conscientious reading of my manuscript and invaluable suggestions concerning it; a writer is not often fortunate enough to find a critic who is just in his evaluations and more and more diverting as his strictures increase. Mary Raines, a gifted nongeographer, who forced me by her frenzied marginal notes of "Where are we now?" to be far more definite than I was in my first draft, was also most helpful. Mr. and Mrs. Ace Comstock and Mr. and Mrs. H. A. de Veber were good enough to pass on their particular chapters; and Miss Anastasia Van Burkalow of the American Geographic Society checked for me the few pages of geology which I ventured upon.

In finding out something about western Canada, I wandered as waywardly in the literary field as we did, on our journey, in the geographic. I would like to mention especially my debt to the following books: For early accounts of the country, Macoun's *Manitoba and the Great North West*, and *Letters of Travel in the North-West* by James Trow; the first volume, *The Geographic Setting*, of Macintosh's classic *Prairie Settlement*; *The Unknown Country* by Hutchison, for its picture of present-day Canada; *The Rocky Mountains*, a popular work on geology by Wallace Atwood; Seton's *Lives of Game Animals*; Anthony's *The Fieldbook of North American Mammals*; Garretson's

vii

The American Bison; *The Moose Book* by Merrill; Hornaday's *Camp-fires in the Canadian Rockies* and *The American Natural History*; *Birds of Western Canada*, by Taverner; *The Canvasback on a Prairie Marsh*, Hochbaum; Kortwright's *Ducks, Geese and Swans of North America*; Armstrong's *The Fieldbook of Western Wild Flowers* (though it deals with the flora of the southwest far more than the northwest). The pamphlets and booklets on the national parks, published by the Canadian government, were of the greatest help; also *The Geology of the National Parks of Canada in the Rockies and Selkirks*, published by the Department of Mines and Resources, *Forestry in Canada*, by the Department of Trade and Commerce, and *The History and Present Status of Wheat Production* by the Department of Agriculture.

Contents

Foreword

ONE morning in early spring the fresh call of its sunlight made us open our windows and step out on our small stone balcony. The day was carved from blue crystal; each detail of Manhattan's intricate design stood fine-edged; a north wind, delicately cold, was a challenge and a delight.

"Canadian air!" I said, intoxicated by its clarity.

"Why do we put up with these small samples?" Lee asked. "Why don't we go up where they make the stuff?"

That is what we did, and this is a book about our holiday. We went simply because Lee said he could not paint one more wildlife picture until he had a chance to see wild country once again—but we found such enjoyment it seemed a shame not to share the natural beauty and the wild things who became our friends.

For two months and more we wandered across the three prairie provinces and up and down the Canadian Rockies, for this was a part of our continent that we did not know at all. In fact, I suddenly realized that I was not sure whether Saskatchewan was between Manitoba and Alberta or between Alberta and British Columbia.

We had seen the coast of British Columbia. Lee when he went up the Inside Passage to Alaska on the *Morrissey* with Captain Bob Bartlett one summer, and I when I traveled to Prince Rupert to meet him. We had spent several vacations in eastern Canada, around the Gaspé when that famous shore road was first opened, about Quebec and up to Tadoussac, in Algonquin Park and Ottawa, and in our beloved canoe country on the border between Ontario and Minnesota. But except once when we had crossed the Rockies by train and spent a week in the Lake Louise region, the interior of western Canada was a totally new field.

We are more grateful than we can say to the many Canadians who made our journey such a delightful one. And any derogatory remarks about towns or roads are not to be taken too seriously—it may have been my own mood, or an accidental occurrence which brought them on. Then too, Canada is growing up so fast that the roads I speak of as gravel may be hard ones now, and villages be modern cities by the time this book is printed. But I hope not—I like western Canada as it is.

Canadian Spring

There was a glimpse of a gray-green river, flooding between cut-banks lined with rosy-budded maples. "There's the Assiniboine," Lee said, "the first of the Canadian rivers we'll follow. That's not a bad name either—Assiniboine. It sounds like the north."

"And there's our welcome to the west—a meadow lark," I cried. Lee stopped the car; and we heard once again, to our keen delight, the fresh fluting notes of the western meadow lark. This song is one which most strongly stirs us, for it recalls all of childhood's springs. It is not at all the simple phrase, *spring o' the year,* which the eastern meadow lark gives; its melody, beginning in sunlight and ending in a rainy cadence, poignant with spring's promise, *is* April.

It rang about us now, all the way to Portage la Prairie. Portage la Prairie—the name comes from the long portage made from the Assiniboine River to Lake Manitoba in the fur-trading days—is the third largest city in Manitoba province. Being inexperienced in meeting Canadian towns, I was surprised at its smallness. But it was an attractive

little place, with its one main street as wide as those of our own western towns, and pleasant homes along the winding river.

From Portage we turned north on a gravel road which was to lead us to Delta and the research station. The level land spread far around us, with occasional farmhouses shielded by clumps of thickset trees. As we bumped along we saw ahead of us, wheeling down on a field, a long flock of small silver birds, close-flying. Snowflakes, Lee said, the same snow buntings we saw on the Gunflint Trail.

Thousands of them glittered across our road, like scurrying snowflakes indeed. As they swirled they showed a pattern of snowy wings and black-striped bodies; then, turning back to silver filagree, they alighted in such a close-tangled mass that the earth vanished from sight. The birds at the rear kept floating over to alight in front of the main flock and this constant drift of pale wings made a lovely shimmering.

All at once, with a subdued murmur, the great flock floated straight up into the air and lit on the telephone wires in such tight ranks that the wires looked heavily frosted. "Why, they're a snowstorm in reverse," I exclaimed.

Now the fields began to revert, with no special demarcation, into marsh grass. Far off we caught a glimpse of blue water. Suddenly a dark line of birds rose in the air above it, wheeled down behind a shore, and dropped into an unseen pond, in the wild abandon of flight that only wildfowl know. We drove along with mounting excitement.

We were driving, as we had since we left Winnipeg, on flat prairie which had long ago been the bottom of Lake Agassiz. Once larger than all the Great Lakes put together, it shrank, as the Ice Age passed, leaving lakes Winnipeg, Manitoba, and Winnipegosis as its last remnants. As the waters slowly receded the swampy country became home for millions of waterfowl, and then changed to prairie except for a strip of marsh near the lake.

And now we came to a welcoming committee. In a deep ditch ran along our road we found our first ducks. Spirited mallards

before us; baldpates lifted small silver crowns; and pintails, exquisites of the old school, stood at their elegant ease. Shovelers, in bright nuptial plumage of cinnamon and green and white, pushed their wide bills through the water.

"They beat us out here after all," said Lee. We had wanted to see the great migrations come up from the south, but spring had been exceptionally early. We had hoped against hope that the wildfowl might be unavoidably detained; here they were, however, already looking very much at home.

We caught our first glimpse of Delta. It was a fishing village, a straggle of small shacks and houses along a narrow ridge whose wind-blown trees separated the marsh from Lake Manitoba. By a pond stood the general store, half-hidden by gnarled willows whose twigs shone vivid orange against the misty lake beyond. It seemed a strange place for fishermen, for though nets were spread on the grass and draped across fences and sheds, there were no boats about.

We crossed a long wooden bridge which led over an inlet and followed a winding road along the marsh to the research station.

The Delta Waterfowl Research Station had always seemed a fascinating venture to us. It originated when James Ford Bell of Minneapolis, becoming much concerned when the droughts started in 1930

1.

Manitoba Marsh

THERE was a marsh in Canada, on the southern shore of Lake Manitoba. It was a large marsh; its shallow bays of harebell blue, its islands of roughly gilded reeds stretched out for miles until they changed imperceptibly into level prairie. Here were wildfowl; here was tranquillity. This was the haven we had long desired.

For we are marsh-lovers and we had been away from the marshes too long. We had a sense of being starved for them, as music-lovers feel the lack of music.

But a Manitoba marsh sounded strange and wild to me. When I first heard of our invitation to the waterfowl research station, seventy-five miles west of Winnipeg, it seemed too remote for our consideration. Nevertheless, one April morning we found ourselves driving toward the place through a flat prairie country where ploughing with four-horse teams was just beginning.

" 'All the winds of Canada call the ploughing-rain,' " I quoted. " 'Take the flower and turn the hour—' " I looked expectantly at Lee, but he does not like Kipling and did not know the end of the quotation.

"I think Canada has as beautiful a name as any country in the world," I went on. "All the more so because nobody seems to know where it came from. And it gives you so much more range than a practical name like United States!"

and ducks began to decrease alarmingly, built a duck hatchery which Edward Ward operated. Here, for more than a decade, more ducks were raised than were bagged on the marsh.

Then Mr. Bell decided that science should come to the aid of the wildfowl, and joined forces with the American Wildfowl Institute. In 1938 Albert Hockbaum, who had studied ornithology at Cornell and game management at Wisconsin, was brought to Delta to do research.

The result was Al's book, *The Canvasback on a Prairie Marsh*, published by the American Wildlife Institute in 1944. The book received universal praise, a rare tribute to such an original work, and Al was awarded the Brewster Medal for it. Lee, who is restrained in his statements, says firmly it is the best duck book he has ever read. The brilliant work, illustrated by its author, outlines and interprets the habits of ducks while mating, nesting, and rearing young, in such a vivid direct way that it holds the attention of anyone interested in birds whether he is a scientist or not.

Since we had admired the book so much we were eager to know the writer, and his associate Peter Ward as well. We had met them both in New York, but only briefly.

Al was a big fellow, generous and kindly. With his vivacious wife Joan, and his two small and sturdy boys, he lived in a rambling cottage across the road from the hatchery. Peter—tall, blond, and gay-spirited—and his wife and little daughter (who were also blond and gay, though not so tall) lived next door to the Hochbaums, with a garden between the two houses.

Then came several small buildings which had once been used for raising mink. Now one was used as an office and as a studio as well, for both Al and Pete were painting wildfowl. In another, made over into narrow but pleasant living quarters, surprisingly decorated with Melanesian trophies, lived Lyle and Grace Sowls, an attractive couple

5

who had come only a fortnight before to join the research staff and study the territorial behavior of the ducks.

Al showed us to our room—two small fishing shacks, or cabooses, as they are called in Manitoba. I had always longed to live on a house-boat and these were closely akin, for they could be pulled anywhere across the marsh. They were tiny things, one a kitchen and one a

bedroom; living in them was like keeping house in a couple of shoe-boxes. Our windows looked out on the marsh, and in the blue air above our roofs the ducks flew over.

As soon as our belongings were indoors, Al took us on a tour of inspection. To the west of our house was a pond where wildfowl were kept wing-clipped for study purposes. From here came gabbling

and quacking all day long. There was also the big hatchery where in the breeding season the incubators popped forth baby ducks of many kinds, as well as other avian infants, from coots to pelicans, to live in an atmosphere of espionage and erudition. Back of the pond, on the edge of the bay, a watch tower stood.

We climbed this tower to get the lay of the land. Here, for the first time, I really saw the marsh. It was an extent of cane, bulrushes, and cattails, its color changing from silver-gilt to deep orange (only for two months of the twelve is it green), broken by large lakes and small ones with channels cut from one to the next. Beyond the windy expanses of Cadham Bay, this tattered gold, broken by glints of liquid blue, swept for miles about us. Only on the horizon was it broken, by the groves of faraway trees.

And it brought to me immediately the same happy serenity that marshes have always given. It is strange, the deep appeal marsh country has for me—those of Long Island, Barnegat, and Maryland; the salt marshes of the Low Country in Carolina; Lanier's marshes of Glynn. There is a special bond, which I cannot explain. For I am prairie-born, and there were no marshes in my childhood. Some ancestor, whose blood is strong in me, must have been a marsh dweller. And then, of course, Lee first showed me marshes.

One of the things I hold against the human race is their determination to do away with marshes; the more wild and beautiful they are, the more someone is possessed to drain and destroy them. Though I would not destroy the human race, I could cheerfully do away with their peculiar values.

I think I love marshes all the more because they do not always disclose their great beauty. They may seem quite unremarkable, and then at a windy touch or a change of light they shake your heart with glory. Some landscapes give themselves to you as you do to them, and I have always felt this in marsh country. There is a reciprocity, a buoyant joy between us.

Now here it was, strong and clear, as the great airy tides washed across the level expanses, like an impalpable sea surging about us. I had been almost afraid I might not recapture it. But I should have remembered our favorite quotation from Burroughs' journals: "Joy in the universe and keen curiosity about it all—that has been my religion. As I grow older, my joy and my interest in it increases." That is so reassuring!

Here, I told myself contentedly, leaning against the rail, is the same winged feeling I've always had in a marsh. How wonderful that it does not change. One thing I have missed fiercely since I've grown up —I never knew of anyone else confessing it—is *running*, the delicious sensation a child has of feeling as light as a leaf in the wind. That is why this marsh feeling of release is more than ever treasured. And really, what a good argument for immortality: the fact that one's spirit keeps on wanting to run and leap—

"Wake up!" said Lee in my ear. "I drove you two thousand miles to see ducks, and now you aren't looking at them."

Scattered about the bay below us floated ducks of many species. I felt a little hesitant; it had been so long since I'd seen wildfowl. Would I ever get them straightened out again? Al and Lee were spinning off identifications at a great rate: canvasbacks, redheads, scaup, ring-necks, gadwalls—oh, gadwalls had to be here, did they? I never recognized gadwalls. Well, today I'd enjoy them just as ducks; I'd sort them out tomorrow.

I turned to the north, where beyond our small cabooses and the research station, the long sandy ridge with its tangles of budding trees hid the lake's shore. Lake Manitoba, Al said, was a hundred and fifteen miles long, larger than Great Salt Lake, but very shallow. Here at its southern end it was a broad and empty surface, without the many islands which it has in the north. The fresh sharp wind came from there, and the sound of the waves against the beach was loud around us.

To the west the village lay. And now I learned why there were

9

many nets and few boats. The inhabitants of Delta are fishermen who fish only in the wintertime, putting their nets out under the ice. They chop a hole and lower a jigger which runs under the frozen floor, knocking against the undersurface. When the fishermen decide it is out far enough, they chop another hole and lift the jigger up, dragging out the far end of the rope to which it is attached. Then a net, tied to the near end of the rope, is pulled out full length under the ice.

Working out on the windy ice all day with the freezing dripping nets is a bleak task, though Al said they did not go out in a fierce gale or if the thermometer was more than forty below! These men have had a hard struggle for existence; the winter just past, however, had brought them comparative fortunes. We could see, from the tower, small cottages ashine for the first time with clean new paint.

We climbed down from the tower, and after an early dinner Peter

drove us east on the sandy ridge road. Pete was just back from the Royal Canadian Air Force, and his joy at returning to the marsh had not lost its first edge. His zest at seeing game showed itself when we began to see the marsh deer, who live in the tall canes, as they came out to feed along the road.

Two does bounded off ahead of us and disappeared into the marsh, making a great leap of pure joy now and then. A fawn ran off like a racehorse, and later we saw a buck watching us from a cluster of yellow cane that stood tall and delicate above the short grass of a burning.

It was sunset now, and over the ridge we saw a flock of geese flying to the lake. Snowdrifts still lingered in the wood, shadowed darkly; usually at this time of year the whole ridge road was deeply drifted, Pete told us, and we felt grateful for the early spring which had cleared

it. Ice lay along the shore and floated in long white rafts on the shallow water. Lee said he had seen the Arctic Ocean look exactly like this.

The color was intense. The water just before us was bright azure and carnation pink; the floating ice floes changed from violet to strong powder blue, through lavender to deep turquoise; the sky was stippled with rose and gold. And in this glory, flock after flock of Canada geese and smaller white-fronts were drifting. I was glad we had come to Manitoba.

2.

Wild Swans in April

WE PASSED Peter on the path to the inlet. "Spring is really here," he said. "The yellow-headed blackbirds came in this morning."

"There they are now," Al exclaimed. "Don't they look like a flock of dandelions!" Up from the canes rose scores of the birds, their orange-gold heads and breasts such a brilliant contrast to their black plumage that they made the marsh grass almost colorless.

My spirits were as light as flying dandelions, too, for this first morning was April at her fairest, and we were to go out in a canoe, which I prefer to any means of travel in this world or above it.

Out into the sharp light of the morning we slipped through the ripples of Cadham Bay, and I was hard put to be the quiet luggage (which sounds better than baggage) in the center of the canoe. Once more afloat, on blue water with golden cane around us and ducks flying in the wind—that is all we need for complete happiness.

But though the marsh looked like a haven of peace, it soon began to sound like a rehearsal for a witches' Sabbath. Wild yells that made me jump and a weird hilarity mixed with wails and howls were the grebes, Al said. Clucks, gulps, and deep *pump-a-chunks* came from bitterns, or thunderpumps, as they are sometimes called. The coots gave such an assortment of croaks, squawks, and cries that I never came to the end of them; blackbirds, besides a musical *o-kee-lee*, produced rusty wheezes;

13

rails were railing and rattling. These hidden birds were as mad with spring as March hares are supposed to be.

In fact, the whole nineteen miles of marsh was one delirious turmoil; the April sun had gone to everyone's head. All around us the wildfowl were in an ecstasy of motion. I have always loved them for their vitality, but now in the midst of the courtship season their fervor was heightened to intoxication.

The place was filled with the gayest carnival spirit. These birds were alert, but not with fear or precaution as they are in the hunting season. On the water the drakes, in gorgeous nuptial plumage, performed their courtship antics and challenged their rivals. And the air was full of courting parties, flying in the wind. Al's canvasbacks streaked by like rust-tipped arrows, mallard pairs flushed from the reeds and stubby scaups floated off before us. I did not know where to look first.

"See those pintails?" Lee exclaimed. "Did you see him fly in front of her, just to display his wing pattern?" But I had my eye on shovelers courting in the water, lifting their peculiar bills and raising and lowering their heads. They courted in a placid way; they did not seem as excitable as most of the ducks.

"A pair of redheads getting up!" Al said. "Watch this—he'll try to catch her tail feathers. Canvasbacks do this too. There—did you see him?" No, I didn't but at least Lee hadn't either.

"Canvasbacks near the point," Lee muttered. "There's the performance Al wrote up—" As I turned, they took to the air in a furious pursuit flight, the female in front, half a dozen males close after her. However she twisted and wheeled, they were just behind. Down she went again and without the least slackening of speed, dove under the water, the drakes still following.

When she came up she began to preen and the drakes gave her a short respite. Then I saw one throw back his head till its top touched his back, and snap it forward. This seemed to start the others off. They

14

stretched their necks high, threw back their heads, and their eyes brightened to ruby. One took the sneak position with his head and neck flat on the water, threatening a rival. We could just hear the low courting notes.

In a sheltered nook the small blue-winged teal were having a reception, all bowing together like little diplomats. Occasionally they took a swift erratic flight together and then landed to resume their bowing. Near by, a pair of gadwall circled side by side, touching bills now and then, in a contented blissful state. I felt slightly disillusioned, however, when they went ashore and the female was forced to defend herself against the advances of two bachelors, while her male, quite oblivious, went on quacking in low and tender tones.

Small buffleheads appeared, and their black and white plumage was very striking. The male's head was iridescent black with a large and flashy triangle of white; it was easy to see, as he puffed it out to twice its size, why his name is a corruption of buffalo-headed.

Though they looked heavy for their small size they rose swiftly and easily from the water. Sometimes they came up from under the surface of the bay, shooting up into the air at full speed. During their courtship antics, the males flew up and then lit standing, to make a long glide as if they were sliding on ice, before they splashed into the water.

15

Then they swam about among the hens, raising their bills, shaking out their crests, and generally showing off like small boys.

"Teal coming in," Lee greeted his small favorites, just as Al mentioned that mergansers were out in front, with the drakes all jockeying for position. I saw neither—I was watching redheads.

The hen redhead seemed to be an aggressive and modern damsel. She was displaying in much the same way that drakes do, jerking her head up and down until a male returned the gesture. She was fickle in her attentions, biting gently at one or another of her swains, teasing them, and generally acting in a most reprehensible manner, though Al said that after mating she settles down into the demure behavior that the other female ducks assume.

The flock suddenly rose into the air. "Oh!" I cried loudly, "I saw him! That redhead—he caught her tail-feathers!"

"Good for you," said Al. "Lots of people never do see that trick—it happens so quickly."

Leaving the wide waters of the bay we pushed through narrow channels out into the marsh. A bittern was making the queer noise which is called stake driving, and then we caught sight of him, standing on bent cattails. Except for his grass-green legs he looked exactly like a broken stick, and I wondered why he didn't choose to resemble a post as long as he could make a sound like driving one.

But he was not immobile. He began to creep forward, in slow motion, putting down his feet very carefully, as if he were in a spy story. When he saw us he felt all was discovered, and made a clumsy escape into the air, flying off with a croak, his feet dangling and his wings beating in a frustrated fashion. A teal came along behind him, shadowing him.

"The ducks are three weeks early at least. I'm sorry you missed the main migration flight," Al said regretfully. "But it was not as spectacular as usual. This is a bad duck year."

16

Heavens, I thought, what would a good duck year be like? This was dizzy enough for me.

Somewhere in front of us we heard a babble of high-pitched cries, half-trumpeted, half-yelled. Ahead of us in the marsh were wild swans! We heard the spatter of their feet along the surface of the lake; and then three whistling swans, their snowy wings beating slowly, rose above the reeds and vanished to the north.

"Hear that low moan?" Al asked us. "That means more of them are about to fly. They moan like that a minute or thirty seconds before they take off."

We came out of the channel into open water and saw a great flock of floating birds, as dazzling white as if they had been carved from snowdrifts. They glided along by the sunlit canes, holding their slender necks straight or at a slight angle, not curved as the domesticated mute swans do.

They looked slim and graceful, although they rank among the largest of our birds and may weigh up to twenty pounds. Some of them were tipping up to feed, heads down and tails up, which seemed an ungainly attitude for birds of such dignity. Ringnecks were swimming about with them, looking very childish, and snatching at the food their great companions brought up from the depths.

"What are the swans feeding on?" Lee asked.

"Sago pondweed," Al said. "They gouge great holes in the underwater beds and pull up tons—really tons—of the plant. Sago is also a favorite food of the ducks, and all my life I've heard hunters complain that swans should be killed off so there would be more food for ducks. But we've found that the beds the swans do not touch may thrive for a few years, and then they disappear or are crowded out by some less desirable plant—milfoil, for instance—while the finest, healthiest, most thriving beds of sago are where the swans feed. We've come to believe that the annual working over the sago beds get each year from the

17

swans is a sort of cultivation and is the reason for their good condition."

Five of the snowy birds lifted their great wings and ran along the water against the wind before rising into the air. In flight their necks stretched out for more than half their total length, so that the long white triangular wings looked curiously far back. More and more flew

over us, and the lifting shimmering birds made me feel as if I were afloat in the wind too; it was hardly a vicarious experience.

Now another group came in from the lake and alighted without the slightest splash, as if they were made of thistledown. The whole flock kept up a constant discussion, murmuring, giving laughterlike hoots and soft calls, or loud single notes in various keys.

Closer to us, a group of swans rose from the water, and their wings sounded like great blankets flapping in the wind. Four came past in a courtship flight, and one made a sudden angry dive at another, who escaped by a quick sideslip which was remarkable in so big a bird.

Al said afterwards that he had seen this mentioned only once in descriptions of the bird, when Seton wrote, in *The Arctic Prairies*, "Flocks of swans flew overhead. . . . 12 were the most in one flock. In this large flock I saw a quarrel. No. 2 turned back and struck No. 3, his long neck bent and curled like a snake. Both dropped several feet, then 3, 4, and 5 left that flock. I suspect they were of another family."

I never saw a swan angry except on this single occasion, but Al said he had seen swans "haul off and give each other real honest-to-goodness knockout blows." He thought the two swans they had found with broken wings were injured in the fights the birds have during courtship, for if they had been shot in the fall hunting season they could not have wintered over, and there is not much chance of hunters wounding them in spring.

I had read an account of a fight between Canada geese in the courtship season, when two males buffeted each other for half an hour or more with their powerful wings, making each other reel under the lashing blows; finally the victor caught his enemy's head in his bill and shook it so ferociously that the victim fled in confused dismay when at last he managed to escape. But to have the swans' serenity lost in such fisticuffs was more entertaining, somehow.

These whistling swans are now increasing in America, but slowly, since they do not breed until their third year. The birds mate for life and seem to have a strong marital devotion. In the research station pond, for instance, there was a wing-clipped female; and her mate, though free, did not go north with the rest of the flock, but stayed all season in the near-by bay.

"We won't go in there and put the swans up," Al said. "I'm afraid if they all fly they might take off for the Arctic. They're due to leave

any day now." We crossed the bay and entered the wide curve of a creek.

Bulrushes and cattails were repeated, in wavering zigzags, in the clear water, and pairs of redheads flushed from the reeds or swam before us. The redhead was a duck I had rarely seen, but I had no trouble in distinguishing it from the canvasback it is supposed to resemble, for its crimson head is round and innocent looking, not the sharp sagacious profile of the canvasback.

This creek was a favorite haunt of the redheads. It was to be the favorite haunt of the Jaques too; of the whole marsh we came to love it best. But at the time we were distracted from its beauty by the coots.

Coots always seem like half-witted Pierrots to me, with chalk-white masks plastered to their silly black heads. But they outdid themselves this morning, splattering before the canoe on their big clownlike feet, their faces rigid with a comic dismay, falling down, picking themselves up and falling down again as they tried to escape us by running among the broken cattails.

We had our lunch here. The creek was a pale gold place; the tall fluffed tops of the phragmites swayed above us, and geometry problems done in gilt bulrushes were all around us. Faint waves gurgled and plopped through the stems that walled us in. We could hear the high voices of the swans and little gusts of air brought a chill April sweetness. Although it was the middle of the day, the duck courting parties still dipped above us, with none of the wariness of other seasons.

After lunch we took our way to Windy Landing, four or five miles east of the research station. As we went along Al was telling us of the many people who had loved this marsh, and we were excited to hear that Lord Grey, who had shown us English birds, once visited here. He, and King George (then the Duke of York) had stayed at the lodge. We asked about Flee Island, which our map had shown to be south of the marsh, and Al said that Sitting Bull had retreated there when his warriors were finally defeated, after Custer's last stand.

Peter met us at the Landing with the car, and we left the canoe on the bank. A rough road led us through the marsh to the ridge where the Manitoba maples (we know them as box elders), twisted and bent from the lake winds, and deeply rosy with their tasselled flowers, made decorative arches above the road. They looked almost like autumn trees except for their extreme fragility. Enormous silver pussy willows prowled up and down willow stems and spangles of orange catkins danced before our eyes.

On the way back we saw many groundhogs; one black one had climbed into a treetop, like a porcupine. Snowshoe rabbits were on the ridge, and jack rabbits in the marsh. And there was a maddeningly self-confident skunk who wandered leisurely down the road ahead of us.

He might be the same one, Pete said, who had haunted the road last fall. An Englishman, garbed in tweeds and a grouse cap pulled down front and back, was driving furiously down the road one day, accompanied by his handsome and taciturn Indian guide, when this skunk

22

appeared in his path. It was too late to stop, so on the driver sped. "My God, Jim," he cried to the Indian, "did that skunk hit us?" "No, Mr. Howell," said the guide; "he didn't lead you enough."

We stopped the car at a curve and walked over to Lake Manitoba to see if the geese were still there. The mid afternoon was warm and a queer light pervaded it. All day there had been smoke in the air from the burning stubble fields (why can't Canada learn from our mistakes and not burn the precious substance of her soil, I wailed to myself) but that wouldn't account wholly for this peculiar atmosphere. "I know," said Pete, "the radio last night told about tremendous dust storms in Alberta; they are just getting to us."

Coming out from the dark shadowed ridge through dense and broken reeds to the shore, we saw swans floating on water of forget-me-not blue. The ice floes had vanished; instead a hundred or more swans made snowy rafts against the blue mist. Blue mist so pervasive that you could not tell where the lake ended and the sky began, so that the birds might have been swimming in the sky or flying under water.

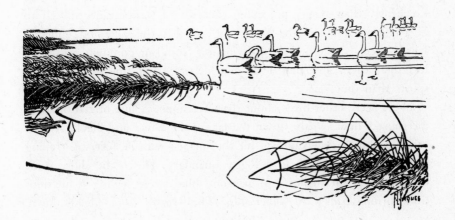

For some atmospheric reason the proud wild things looked gigantic as they drifted along, their slim necks erect, their small heads with the ebony bills very regal; and their faint reflections might have been white clouds floating low in the sky. It seemed the vision of some mystic; it had an ethereal, another-world look, all the more so because it was early afternoon.

One swan drank from the lake, with his neck curled into a circlet. Five or six, one with a darker head, came floating past in a row, each swimming dreamily with one foot, their wake a taut silver line behind them. They cried out continually in high single notes, bittersweet.

I wondered if these high clear notes had been the source of the ancient swan song legend. But they were far from a lament—they bore out, rather, Socrates' noble words before he drank the cup of hemlock: "Men, through their own fear of death, belie the swans too, and say that they, lamenting their death, sing their last song through grief, and they do not consider that no bird sings when it is hungry or cold or is afflicted with any other pain, not even the nightingale, or swallow, or the hoopoes, which they say sing lamenting through grief. But neither do these birds appear to me to sing through sorrow, nor yet do swans; but in my opinion, belonging to Apollo, they are prophetic, and foreseeing the blessings of Hades, they sing and rejoice on that day more excellently than at any preceding time. But I too consider myself to be a fellow-servant of the swans and sacred to the same god, and that I have received the power of divination from our common master no less than they, and that I do not depart from this life with less spirits than they."

There were other birds about that afternoon. A line of red-breasted mergansers flew swiftly down the lake, very white and black. A loon came in, sailing down until it hit the surface with its feet still trailing behind it as if it were in a foggy quandary. Down the shore some Canada geese, in shallows of peacock blue, were having a hilarious time turning backward somersaults. They really were. Heads down,

24

heels (if geese have heels) over, they had forgotten their dignified demeanor and were romping like a gang of schoolboys.

I had always thought that Canada geese were almost too serious-minded, they had such a reputation for wariness and sagacity to maintain. It was a joy to see them frolicking about. We watched them for a long time.

But when I think of that afternoon it is always the floating dream-like quality that I remember.

3.

Delta Acquaintances

During our first week at Delta, April changed to May and the weather remained balmy and delicate, more like Maryland air than Manitoba. We spent day after day seeing the marsh.

I became aware of grebes at this time. The only previous contact I had ever had with them was with the small pied-billed, and that was slight (both the contact and the grebe). As I traveled around with wild-fowl enthusiasts, we sometimes came to a pond or lake with one small black speck in the center; and I was always crying triumphantly, "There's a duck!" The reply, nearly always, was a bored, "It's only a grebe." Why *only* a grebe? Hath not a grebe eyes? Hath not a grebe organs, dimensions, affections? If you prick him, does he not bleed? I was sorry for grebes, each one a solitary little figure, unregarded.

But here they were conspicuously together, and I grew extremely interested in them, though I never had the warm affection for them that I have for ducks. They must be cold-blooded themselves, for they rank nearest to the reptiles from which birds spring, and are among the most aquatic of our birds. Their plumage is hardly like feathers; hairy above and silky beneath, it is compact and completely waterproof.

It is not hard to distinguish them from ducks; their bodies are flatter, the necks very narrow, their tails only absurd hairlike tufts. Their feet, triple paddles instead of the single ones the ducks have, are used with great rapidity. Grebes have several peculiar ideas, one of which is to eat their own feathers; they carry a large mass of them around in their stomachs.

At this time we saw four kinds out of a possible five. The largest, the western grebe, had not yet arrived. But we often saw the Holboell's, almost as large, in spite of the fact that he is supposed to be the

shyest of the water birds. He was dark and handsome in his breeding plumage, his snowy cheeks and black cap puffed out so that they looked amazingly large for the slim neck of bright crimson. The Holboell's love song was the eeriest of all the marsh cries. I never got used to it. It began with wild piercing cries of anguish and then trailed off into melancholy wailing; you would never think he was of a retiring nature from the way he expresses himself vocally.

The horned grebe is smaller than a teal, but in the courtship season it shrieks almost as loud as the Holboell's. At that time it adorns itself with two orange crests, one on each side of its nape, and goes in for large black ruffs on its cheeks, so that its head looks very bushy on its thin neck. It is not at all timid and delights in rough water and stormy weather.

27

The eared grebe is even smaller and his short bill seems to tilt up, making him look very impertinent. For his courting he has sprays of hairy gold feathers that fan back from behind his small eyes in a sprightly way, and a black crest which stands up on the top of his head and gives him a look of great surprise.

Last of all comes the dark pied-billed, quite babyish in appearance and often called dabchick. It is also called hell-diver, since when it dives it may come up with only the bill above the surface of the water, which confuses the spectator into thinking it is still below and makes him suspect the bird.

We often watched them, as well as the ducks, from the canoe. When it was too windy for canoeing, we explored the small lanes which led to the south edge of the marsh. We always found many ducks in the ditches along the road and in the shallow sloughs. The prairie grass was full of slender pintail necks, pair by pair, and Lee found two pintail nests, one in a meadow where the long bleached grass lay in swirls, and another in a field which had been cleared by burning off the stubble. Here a pair of pintails were staying staunchly by their scorched eggs. These eggs would never hatch, of course, and a pintail brood was lost through such misplaced loyalty.

Shovelers had already staked out their territories along the ditch in some places; it was quite disconcerting to find what a sense of possession birds have regarding real estate. The drakes defend their land fiercely against others of their own kind, though they teach us a lesson by sharing areas peaceably with ducks of other species.

I was surprised to read in *The Canvasback on a Prairie Marsh* that territory does not mean nesting site, and that just any water area will not serve. A duck's territory is very specialized: it must have food and water, a loafing spot, and nesting cover near at hand, though the nest as a rule is located beyond the boundaries of the territory. The loafing spot is indispensable. Here the pair rest and preen together, and here the drake waits for the hen while she is on the nest. Somehow, this loafing spot makes ducks more than ever akin to us.

Al pointed out to us how easily we could tell the courtship flights here, when the drakes all pursue the hen and ignore each other, from the flights to protect territory, when the resident drake flies up indignantly to drive off an encroaching pair. The fact that the drake is defending his home seems to give him a moral advantage; he is practically always victorious.

The prairie sloughs had ducks of many kinds, often migrants—teal, pintails, baldpates, mallards, and gadwall—mixed in happy confusion. I was recognizing ducks without thinking them out now, just as one recognizes human friends; it took daily contact to bring that about. I even took to identifying the birds by their method of flight, without seeing the color pattern, and was extremely pleased with myself.

Along these roads we often saw great flocks of blackbirds feeding, though the colonies nested in the canes close to open water. We saw one huge congregation. Their black bodies hardly showed against the black earth; only the yellow heads went hopping along the plowed field, all facing the south wind. They looked more than ever like runaway dandelions, or perhaps marigolds this time; when they all flew up together, the white patches on their wings were as striking as the

golden heads, and, with the glittering black wings, made a gorgeous frieze against the blue air.

These birds were so brilliant I expected an equally glorious song, perhaps like the English blackbirds'. The bird gave a preliminary note or two—not bad. Then he made a tremendous effort, swelling up, stretching his neck, opening his mouth wide, and spreading out his tail feathers. All set—but out came only a hoarse squawk. He looked confused, and tried again, over and over, but he never succeeded in getting it any better.

I remember particularly the anticlimax of this song, but Taverner in *Birds of Western Canada* describes the noise itself in detail: "Climbing stiff-leggedly up a reed or tule stalk, the male, with wings partly raised, lowers his head as if about to become violently ill, and disgorges a series of rough angular consonants, jerkily and irregularly, with many contortions and writhings, as if their sharp corners caught in the throat and they were born with pain and travail. They finally culminate . . . in a long-drawn, descending buzz, like the slipping of an escapement in a clock spring."

In late afternoon we often saw the short-eared owls flying low across the prairie grass. They flew in slow motion and their wings had the widest possible arc—a hundred and eighty degrees. In the courtship flight the wings came together both above and below the body, and once we saw an owl touch them several times under him without lifting them over his back—a special gallant touch, I suppose, like bowing from the waist.

Now the plowed fields were just wondering if they'd try a green misty look. The trees in the "bluffs" (as they call the groves in western Canada) were a subtle orange-green, while the willow branches were a bright lemon color. There was the fragrance of tender leaves; everything was immaculately clean; even the little breezes were newly made. Mirages swam in the pale sky—a farmhouse with its trees seemed to float on a small island, and two elevators in the distance looked like Mont-Saint-Michel.

Over the prairie came the distant booming of prairie chickens. The saskatoon, a shadbush which is everywhere through the northwest, began to open small silver-gray leaflets to the spring. Meadow larks were riotous from dawn till dusk; at times their clamor was deafening.

One late afternoon after a rain the clouds broke away and the gauzy tatters were lit with sun. The Franklin's gulls, black-capped, their white breasts flushed with faint rose as they are in the spring, had been following tractors down the wet fields, but now they started to the lake. They were flying against a strong north wind, and as we kept pace with them in the car we found them making twenty miles an hour. Against the dark clouds they sparkled like bursts of bright stars from sky rockets.

Buffeted more and more, the long lines came lower, flying over bluffs and farms. Then lower still, just above the plowed earth. They looked as if they were running miraculously fast, and when they came to a fence or a hedge they rose a little, as horses take the hurdles in a steeplechase, and then sank nearly to the earth again. Flying low like this they made from twenty-five to thirty miles an hour.

31

When we came to the ditches the tiny Wilson's phalaropes were there for the first time. These shore birds, as dainty as porcelain miniatures, were whirling round on the surface of the water as if on pivots. Clockwise and counterclockwise they went, bobbing and spinning and darting at invisible prey.

They are most unusual birds. The female is the larger and more brilliantly colored. She is the aggressive one in courtship; she keeps other females away from her man; she, the books say with an air of surprise, makes the most noise. The male broods the eggs, but he cannot do that in his own way; she stays around to oversee the process.

However far we explored, our first choice was still Windy Landing. There we were in the heart of the marsh's life as soon as we pushed the canoe out from shore.

It was best at sunset.

I remember especially one evening with Lyle and Grace Sowls, who were good company in a canoe, being keen ornithologists and blessed with a sense of humor besides. We started when the sun was still above the horizon. The air was delicious, soft and very clear, with a north wind which, incredibly, was a lazy one. The tall canes shone deeply copper in the late light and about them lapped tiny ripples of an intense gentian blue. Gulls made a diaphanous canopy above our heads.

Many ducks were about, two by two. Courting parties were in accelerated tempo. Some of the pursuit flights were so intense and the birds so close-packed that the wings seemed to clash together. We agreed that the pintails took the prize for grace. Their maneuvers were like the perfection of ballet, with beautiful precision and style as a drake, sweeping past the hen, displayed his patterned wings while she arched her slender neck and dipped her bill in a slight but characteristic movement.

We heard the whistle of the yellowlegs, and the thunderpumps were pumping thunder in a practiced manner. "Look at that ugly coot," said Grace, "with her wake like a golden bridal veil spread out behind her."

When translucent light broke in strong rays from a gray-gold cloud behind which the sun was hidden, and wild swans flew up against the primrose horizons, the evening turned into poetry. And after sunset we had wide tumbles of pastel clouds, while the wind vanished, so that as the still water flawlessly reflected them it was like floating in clusters of giant bubbles.

I begged for a journey down our winding creek, and we entered its

crystal silence. The only sound was when a subdued bittern made a single clunk, driving a very small post. The creek water was so undisturbed that the arched bulrushes and their reflections made complete circles—gilded circus hoops for the antics of the coot buffoons.

Then, just ahead of us, peace was shattered. Two coots in the reeds were engaged in furious battle. I was never more taken aback. I had always thought of coots as addlepated but good-natured souls, and now these were fighting as viciously as sled dogs do. Breast to breast, they stabbed at each other with their white beaks, rearing back their heads and thrusting forward with fury. They struck underhandedly with their feet as well, and beat at each other with their black wings.

As we watched in fascinated horror one got his adversary down and held him under water with his feet, while he stabbed down with a murderous bill. It was a savage sight. Lee and Lyle thought that perhaps the victim escaped under water, but I think he was drowned then and there.

When we paddled out into the bay again, the reeds on the horizon were a rosy line across looking-glass water. From the blue dusk in the

south we caught sight of a long **V**. Geese on migration, we said, but it turned out to be thirty snow-white pelicans, flying with their black wingtips curled up in the wind and their gold bags under their chins. The nuptial decorations on their bright orange bills were distinct, sticking up like gunsights; one bird was very distinguished, having two of the horny discs. The flock looked, against the high rosy clouds, like birds from the Arabian Nights.

It was high time for us to go home, yet it was impossible to leave. In transparent water of the clearest salmon-pink, wildfowl silhouettes trailed grass-green wakes behind them. Where the creek was shadowed to deep purple, the birds could not be seen and the long silver wakes seemed lines drawn across the dark surface by an invisible hand.

After a while both water and sky were so bleached of color that dark blue clouds and their reflections floated in one round sphere of emptiness. The only change in the airy vacuums above and below was that sleepy ducks were dotted about the lower one and you could not imagine why they did not fall into the infinite abyss beneath them. The water had perfectly reflected the clouds in the sky, but the sky did not reflect the water's sleeping birds—that was the only difference.

In the narrow shadow by a far shore we saw little white fountains of water scurrying along, as invisible coots fled in foolish panic. Grace found the first barb of a star.

"There ought to be a new moon," I said; and we found it just beneath the star in a green afterglow, the merest whisper of a moon, a still small voice. I had that feeling of beauty heightened beyond bearing, which stamps such moments deep into the memory.

In these brief flashes we see the world in a splendor which is usually dimmed by our own preoccupations. These are the moments in which, as Stewart Edward White said, we find ourselves exalted above the ordinary level of existence. "In the special moments, we seem most in balance, most sharply sensitized. Something real, that has been locked away from us by the strange thin screen of personality, rushes through us like a tide."

One never knows when this revealing light will flash—it is not always unusual beauty which calls it out. I remember once walking toward home when the familiar street corner was so glorified in sun and shade that I stood still, transfixed by a sensation of utter inexplicable happiness.

These moments are among the most precious of our possessions; I knew that even when I thought the experience was my own private madness. Now that I have found it is a universal experience I enjoy collecting vivid descriptions of it. Usually in poetry, of course, but John Muir's writings are permeated with it, and Emerson rather surprised me by writing of such an adventure: "Crossing a bare common in snow puddles, at twilight, under a clouded sky, without having in my thoughts any occurrence of special good fortune, I have enjoyed a perfect exhilaration. I am glad to the brink of fear." Many of Katherine Mansfield's letters describe the emotion: "Although life is loathsomely ugly . . . there is something at the back of it all," she says, "which if we were great enough to understand would make *everything*,

everything, indescribably beautiful. One just has glimpses, divine warnings—signs. Do you remember the day we cut the lavender?"

It was idyllic, that evening, but indeed the whole time at Delta was, from the first thing in the morning, when we woke to hear the gulls crying over our rooftree, or a whitethroat's *Canada, Canada*, until we looked at the Great Dipper (not in the north as we were accustomed to see it, but strangely set in the middle of the sky, exactly over our cabooses) before we went in to bed.

Not only did we stay out in the spring weather all day long, but we had such fun with our companions on our expeditions and in between times. Al had a steady dependable look and this did not belie him, but he could also be a mischievous imp. After I was misled into taking a wildlife official for the local minister, so that my apologetic attitude for not attending afternoon service confused the gentleman completely and put me all at sea, I tried to mistrust appearances.

Even our chores were diverting—cleaning lamp chimneys and bringing in wood and water. Lee would drive out to Lake Manitoba with Pete and Al on the tractor to fill the big barrels which held our water supply; Grace and I experimented with local flora for vegetables, using the tiny nettle leaves for spring greens and the new cattail shoots for salad. Mail came to Delta only three times a week, and we often drove into Portage after it, exploring side roads on our way.

It had been agreed before we came that we were to be neighbors and not guests, but there was constant running back and forth between the houses with marsh gossip, and almost every day we were guests at breakfast, lunch or supper, invited by one or another of our "pretty maids all in a row."

This hospitality was fortunate, for the only fly, but a very large one, in the ointment, was my kitchen stove. This was the more maddening because the bedroom stove which Lee tended was a little angel, starting in the morning with no fuss at all, never going out without permission, not even smoking. Whereas my kitchen stove was a fiend in inhuman form.

I wish the author of the spirited essay on "The Total Depravity of Inanimate Objects" could have written a case history of this stove. It was very small and held two pots or pans with difficulty. Since I always needed hot water, being used to a city's inexhaustible supply, a kettle took half this space, which left me with one spot for a cooking utensil.

If you took your eye off that stove for one second, it went out. The only way to fire it was to remove whatever was cooking and take off a stovelid; this had to be done every two minutes, for the firebox was so narrow-minded it refused to hold more than two small sticks at a time. So I performed a continuous juggling act, in which I needed three hands, one to lift the cooking pan, one to take off the iron lid and one to put in the wood. The lid-lifter had the power of becoming invisible at will.

The stove, like a spoiled baby, either refused to eat at all, looking the other way when you tried to poke the wood in, or else it con-sumed it at one gulp and yelled for more. If the weather was cold, so was the stove, like a clam, though it could still give blisters in some mysterious way; if the day was hot the stove suddenly became mother's willing little helper, sending out fiery rays like a cast-iron demon.

I will not go into the subject of dampers.

4.

My Hero

LONG ago in a Louisiana marsh I had the rare experience of falling in love at first sight. The object of my affections was a ruddy duck, stubby and small and fast asleep at that. I saw him for only a few minutes, but I have never forgotten him.

I am not alone in my devotion to him. *Erismatura jamaicensus rubida* is his full name, but he is endowed with far more nicknames that any other duck can begin to claim, and each one testifies to an endearing characteristic. Butterball, blatherskite, toughhead, dumpling duck, god-damn, bumblebee coot, little soldier, stifftail, dinky, sleepy brother, noddy paddy, diptail diver and stub-and-twist are only a few of these.

When I found we were to spend springtime in a marsh, my most fervent hope was that I might see that ruddy duck once more. But when I arrived I was so delighted with the horizontal landscapes and the meeting with old friends—canvasbacks, pintails, mallards, teal—that I forgot my ruddy infatuation completely.

The first morning Lee and I were out alone, however, we paddled our canoe into a little bay where the water was so calm that we could not tell where the reeds ended and their images began. Suddenly something ruffled its surface so that although the reeds still stood quiet and sedate, their reflections shook with secret laughter. Why?

39

The cause came after the effect. Out from the golden stems into the full sunlight came a ruddy duck.

But what a changed ruddy! Not at all the dark, squat, sleepy little bunch of feathers that had once touched my heart. Down south he had worn a winter suit as unassuming as the female's. But now he was resplendent. For he does not merely lose his feathers and go into eclipse plumage as all other ducks do; he follows his own plan in this as in everything else he does, and has a summer costume entirely different from his winter one.

Here he was ruddy indeed, with rich red feathers. He wore a shining black crown which emphasized his snowy cheeks, and he had a bill of dazzling blue. His spiny spike of a tail stood straight up, and as I watched he spread it out into a ridiculous fan. He really was a duck!

As we paddled near he took off, running along the water on his large feet in a desperate effort to get himself into the air. Then he buzzed away, his short wings making him look like an exceptionally large Junebug. "He's gone," I cried sadly. "I did want to see his courtship!" Though ducks of many kinds were everywhere about and their

activities most distracting, I kept my wholehearted watch for that ruddy all morning. But I looked in vain.

In late afternoon we were out in the canoe again. All around us emerald dragonflies were flying over the stands of cattails or stood on gauzy wings, motionless in the air before us, as they regarded us with mild surprise. Over the marsh, gilded in the tranquil light, the wild swans were flying. We could see distant lines of snowy birds coming in from Lake Manitoba and hear their high hornlike calls as they landed on hidden water. As we floated silently along, hunting for their secret haven, there was no sound except for their far-off calls and now and then the weird *pump-a-chunk* of a bittern.

Then, close to a far shore, I suddenly saw six ruddies. Five males and a female—it was a courting party. I forgot all about wild swans. Ruddies! I was so eager to see them that I could hardly focus my field glasses. "Quiet! *Quiet!*" I warned Lee—the only time I ever issued the caution to him instead of the other way round.

I was afraid we would disturb the gathering, but they were far too engrossed. Each male was doing his utmost to attract his lady's attention. Round he would steam, his short neck puffed out and his chin drawn in, jerking his fan tail forward as his head jerked back, so that the two almost touched. He was in such a fiery state that his bright blue bill seemed to send forth sparks and his cheeks blew out like two little puffs of white smoke in his excitement.

If you stop to think how high spring's fever (not to be confused with spring fever) can soar in the human race and how much keener a bird's emotions are, because of his higher metabolism, then consider how of all birds the wildfowl have the greatest zest in life, and of all wildfowl the ruddy duck seethes most with energy—you can judge somewhat of his ardor here.

The female, even smaller than the males, was most demure. In her dark plumage she swam mildly about while the drakes sailed up to each other, full speed ahead, so high in the water that I could see their

41

silvery bellies as they plunged like sea horses at each other, splashing and fighting, with the blessed damosel in the thick of it.

We pushed the canoe deep into the cattails and waited for them to come by. At last one came along, with the air sac in his neck (he is the only duck to have such a silly inspiration) blown up so that he was like a little feathered balloon. He was too filled with passion and air to express himself—he could only say in a choked voice, "Ip–Ip–Ip"; I waited for "Hooray," but it did not come. Besides pushing out his white cheeks he spread snow-white puffs behind his upright tail.

Another ruddy came out of the grasses almost submerged, so that he looked too short to believe. He made you feel cut off, as a very brief answer does. When he came out into the open and saw that all was well, he rose higher, lifting his tail and unfurling it. A hen bobbed up from beneath the water and he turned toward her.

This incensed the first drake. Two little ears rose straight up from his head—curious rabbit ears—and he sailed out to defend the female to the death. The other immediately became nonchalant; he lay down on the water and scratched himself with a casual foot—his tail remaining erect and defiant. Then the trio caught sight of us, and flew off like small mechanical toys; their wings seemed to flap round and round, their feet splashed water: one, two, one, two.

Soon after, a whole flotilla of ruddies floated out from a grassy island and began to display. The drakes were overcome with joy, for their hens had just arrived from the south. (In other species the mated pairs arrive in the marsh first, but the ruddy remains individualistic: the drakes travel together on migration; the hens follow at a later date.) One drake was so distraught that he gave his full display to a dignified canvasback, who ignored him loftily.

Another came along all alone, so low in the water that he looked like a head floating on a feather. These birds have the ability to rise or sink in the water at will. They often disappear, tail first, or sink like

42

a submarine without diving. Sometimes only the head with its bright blue bill will appear above the water surface.

They have great aquatic skill. Lee said he was sure there were twice as many in the bay as we saw; they dived so constantly and were under the surface as much as they were above it. In 1840 Audubon wrote of their ability to stay under water: "I often waded out and pursued them. Then it was that I saw the curious way in which they used their tails when swimming [under water] employing it now as a rudder, and again with a vertical motion; the wings being also slightly opened and brought into action as well as the feet." Being diving ducks and largely vegetarian, they find most of their food on the bottom, and with it they swallow large quantities of sand and gravel.

Their courtship is wholly aquatic; they do not make the swift pursuit flights that other ducks delight in. It seems to be the birds with long pointed pinions who are expert at flying. The ruddies, with their short rounded wings, have a jerky flight, and even on long migrations seldom fly high. They seem always glad to get back to their aquatic element, dropping into the water without the least check in speed, with spray flying about them. On land they are completely helpless.

43

Their legs are so far back that they cannot take more than a step or two without falling on their sky-blue noses.

After this evening in the canoe, ruddies really became an obsession with me. There were birds of many nations about, any of which I would ordinarily have been avid to watch; now I gave them only passing glances.

There were crowds of ruddies—I had never dreamed there were so many in the world—and I *had* to see them all. They would come along in little armadas, all sails set. Tiny, gallant, comic. But not comical as coots are. Coots have always amused me, but they are addlepated clumsy things. A ruddy is a midget d'Artagnan, stouthearted and adventurous, full of fire and spirit and absurdity. I can just see a ruddy starting out into the world for the first time and immediately getting involved with a mallard and a pintail and a canvasback, all at once.

Though they are cunning, they are also admirable. Lee says that hunters find ruddies are difficult to kill. A blue-winged teal, which is about the same size, is a gentle-spirited bird, and dies easily; while a ruddy has the will to live so strong in him that he takes an unbelievable amount of punishment and still survives. I am sure he was once a tough little egg.

For a long time I never saw one who did not look alert and excited, and I began to wonder whether the ruddy's nicknames of sleepyhead, sleepy brother, deaf duck, dumb-bird, and sleepy-jay applied to him only in the languid air of the south, or if I simply failed to see him in quiet or in pensive mood.

However, one stormy afternoon we saw two males bobbing up and down in the rough bay, fast asleep, with their heads tucked into the middle of their backs and looking like Winken and Blinken, each in his little shoe. (Nod was not about.) So we decided that the cold weather sent them back to winter habits and made them sleepyheads, just as it discouraged the other ducks' courtship flights and gave them quiet wintry moods.

44

Once, on Portage Creek, we found more ruddies than we had ever seen before. It was an amazing sight; the ruddy really outdoes all other ducks in his continuous courtship. Here he was, displaying not only before the female, but sailing along by himself, practicing his enchantments and chuckling away at a great rate.

Sometimes he said, with smothered emotion, "chuck–chuck–churrrr," and then more thoughtfully, "Ip–Ip–Ip." They say that there are occasions when, kicking the water and making the spray fly, he also exclaims "Tick–tick–tickety–tock!" but I was never fortunate enough to hear that poetic phrase. The male is as talkative as this only in the courtship season. The female, like many women, is completely silent.

Fifteen drakes came past us in a long line, their bills as blue as bits of summer sky. One drake was slapping his turquoise beak against his chest in an indignant way, another suddenly had an overwhelming impulse to go places and stood straight up, pressing his tail under water and drawing his bill in tight against his breast, to go scooting along the water like a mettlesome speedboat.

One fortunate ruddy had two hens in tow and was filled with an unholy pride. He blew himself up until he nearly burst; his head jerked back and forth and up and down till we expected it to fly off by itself; his tail was proud as a peacock's if not as long; and as he gave his stifled croon, even the feathers on his back bounced vigorously. When

45

another drake came near his lady loves he flew into such a rage he seemed in imminent danger of a stroke.

I had read that when a ruddy challenged a rival "the feathers over the eyes are puffed up into two swollen protuberances like the eyes of a frog and his orbs gleam forth with what appear to be belligerent and baleful glances." And taking this to mean that lumps popped out like eyebrows above his eyes, I looked in vain for the phenomenon. It was not for a long time that I realized this was a description of what I called the rabbit ears, or little horns, that stuck up from the top of his head when he was most enraged.

Sometimes when he was attacking he would put his head flat on the water, submerge his tail, and then, rumpling up his back until it looked more like fur than feathers, so that he had the look of a miniature brown bear, he would rush violently at his rival. When these water fights occurred, the female often opened her bill widely, as if in feminine admiration of such spirited conduct.

The next day we were back again, and when we rounded the curve of the creek we found a hundred or more of my ruddies, in full display.

There never was such a duck for display. Ducks in general court intensely early in the season, when the hen is choosing her mate. The males can't be too gallant, until the female makes her choice. Then there is a period of noncourtship, which must be disconcerting for her after all the attention she had been receiving. When the nest-site is chosen and they are ready to begin raising a family, the drake courts her again. Not nearly as fervently, however, as he did when he was on a competitive basis. Such is life. But the ruddy, bless his heart, remains constantly ardent.

Of course Kortwright in his otherwise admirable *Ducks, Geese, and Swans of North America* says bluntly that ruddies are sullen, ferocious, bad-tempered birds. With this I take violent issue. The ruddy is quick-tempered, but certainly not morose; he is the cavalier type, with his hand on his sword and a laugh in his throat.

And as for being sulky! He is debonaire from morning till night, sometimes far into the dusk after other wildfowl are drowsy and dull. Neither does he flee from companionship; he is in the thick of it, self-reliant and at ease, though the ducks around him may be twice his size. Sullen and ferocious my eye!

I have the strongest affection for this small duck, but not at all the feeling of tenderness that I usually have for little creatures. I think that is because he has such character. Tenderness always includes compassion, if only a drop of it, and you cannot give a ruddy duck compassion. You give him respect and laughter.

The hen ruddy is as unique as the drake, in her quiet way. She and the drake are inseparable. In the brooding season, though he does not help her brood the eggs, at least he is around. No matter how often he may go off on short flights with other young fathers, whizzing about the lake, he comes back sooner or later.

She nests much later than the hens of other species and has the doubtful distinction of laying the largest eggs for her size of any duck. They are larger than those of a mallard or a canvasback, as large as a great blue heron's. Also she will go on indefatigably to lay as many as fifteen or twenty, impossible for such a small mother to cover, so she arranges them neatly in layers in her basketlike nest.

She builds this of reeds or bulrushes, to match the plants around it, and attaches it to the growing stems. It stands seven or eight inches above the water and usually has a sloping runway to it, so it is easy for her to escape from home if she likes.

After the brood hatches, the ruddy drake often takes a great interest in the family. Not always—the ruddies are independent about this virtue too, and at Delta there seems to be a fifty-fifty chance of paternal attention. But it is not an unusual sight to see one swimming at the head of a close-packed line of ducklings, the mother following as rear guard.

47

Even the ducklings differ from those of other species. They dive courageously for their food at the first contact with water, though other small ducks stay timidly, for a time at least, on the surface. It has been found that it is impossible to raise ruddy ducklings in hatcheries. They simply refuse to eat in captivity. And while the new-hatched young of other ducks will nestle down in your hand, this duckling, even at one day old, will try to chew your finger off. That's my ruddy!

5.

The Elk of Riding Mountain

On a May morning which seemed out of *Aucassin and Nicolette* we drove west, the Sowls in their car and Peter with us. Until we came to the first hill we had seen in a long time, at Neepawa, about seventy miles west of Delta, and saw the purple outline of Riding Mountain in the distance, we were still on the level lake bed of vanished Agassiz.

We had seen the southern shore of this ancient lake when we saw the Turtle Mountains of Dakota; its eastern boundary, east of Winnipeg, is the rim of the Laurentian or Pre-Cambrian Shield, composed of the oldest rocks in the world, the great plaque which spreads out around Hudson Bay. Now here was the western shore of the extinct lake.

North from Neepawa about thirty miles a side road led to Riding Mountain Park. Before us an abrupt escarpment lifted eleven hundred feet above the prairie. This mountain's summit is a wooded plateau, which runs west for seventy miles; it has many glacial lakes scattered through its forest. Since 1929, it has been a game refuge of one hundred and forty-eight square miles.

When we came to the park gates there was a sign: CLOSED. Now Rid-

49

ing Mountain has one of the largest herds of wild elk in all Canada, and from the moment I had heard its name I had been so eager to see it that I was sure I never would. "My premonition was right," I said to myself gloomily; "I knew I'd never get there." At which moment a warden appeared to tell us that the park had just been opened.

From the smooth prairie the road began to climb immediately, through a deep forest with the damp scents of jackpine, tamarack, and spruce. There were no green leaves, only buds on the verge of un-furling in brush and thicket. I was glad of these returns to the very beginnings of spring, with marsh marigolds springing out like daylight stars in the black ditch, and the bare twigs of the birches a bright plum color.

At a lookout on the east slope we left the car and climbed a fire tower. Above the forest treetops we looked out on an incredibly wide semicircle of level farmland which had once been a sheet of ice, then a sea of water, and after that a gigantic marsh. Lake Manitoba glinted on the horizon.

The sharp slopes below us were the result of erosion which took place before the Ice Age. From where the tower stood, the Indians must often have looked out over the prairie on vast herds of elk and buffalo. For both the Assiniboine and the Cree nations had fished and hunted here, between battles with the Blackfeet from the west. Through centuries these long ridges had been used as Indian trails.

We built our noon campfire by a pool in the dense spruce forest, and had steaks and hot coffee. Now there were forest birds instead of prairie ones. Chickadees sang their spring songs, and flickers flashed their yellow feathers like sunlight into the shadows. The moosebirds —the whisky-jacks or Canada Jays—took it into their impertinent heads to act shy and aloof. It seemed a strange thing to be surrounded by tangled boughs, alders of deep violet, tamaracks the color of faint moonlight, and black-green spruces, instead of the immense and empty dome of light above the marsh at Delta.

All afternoon we drove along shadowed roads looking for elk, without seeing even a little one. The density of the forest fascinated us and we walked down trails through thick muskeg moss in heavy thickets, and stood still to smell the scent of pine needles warmed by the sun— there is no fragrance in the world which equals that. Once we saw a deer; but never an elk. It was harrowing.

At the little village of Wasagaming on Clear Lake, we separated. The Sowls were going to camp out in the lowlands south of the park and make a count of the ducks nesting in each pothole pond. Peter, Lee, and I decided to follow the north road which ran for forty miles through the park, and stay all night at the town of Dauphin. If we saw no elk in the evening, there would still be a chance next morning, coming back.

"But we'll surely see them tonight," Peter said, rumpling his hair in his eagerness, as we sat on a hill eating our early picnic supper and watching for game to appear in the swamp below us. "Elk don't run around all night the way the deer do; they feed in the evening and the morning. We'll surely see them." He had not been in the forest since before the war and he was frantic to see big game again.

"The lamb," I thought sympathetically. "If only we can find one elk for him . . ."

It was almost sunset when we started north through heavy stands of spruce. And Lee had driven only a few miles when Peter cried, "There's one!" A big animal was moving off through the dim trees, its light-colored rump patch glimmering in the shadow.

"There's another!" Peter spotted it ahead of us as soon as we moved on. We saw this one plainly as it trotted off down a well-worn trail.

Elk began appearing all along our road now, among the aspens, in the brown grass, behind spruce boughs; with twilight coming the splendid creatures had taken over the country. It was theirs as it had been before man appeared on the continent, and we had the feeling that only by special favor were we allowed to pass.

51

These elk were large and handsome, the bulls weighing around seven or eight hundred pounds, the does somewhat smaller. They were brownish gray with dark heads and legs, and the large rump patches were a deep creamy yellow. Pete's hunting fever was so aroused that he could not stay in the car. He kept dashing out to chase elk up a trail or to see if more were beyond a ridge.

The bulls' horns were just beginning to grow and looked as if they were covered with brown moss; some of them were already more than eight inches long. By August they would be fully grown and might have a length of sixty inches. Then the velvet would peel or be rubbed off against trees, and the horn would grow hard. The magnificent antlers are carried all winter; in March they fall off and the miraculous process begins all over again.

As the bulls moved away with their heads high, as if they were withdrawing to let us pass on sufferance, they had such a royal character, such an assured dignity, that the elk we had seen in captivity might as well have been of a different species. These wild things had a pride which was an intrinsic quality; they of all creatures should never be confined, since one of their basic needs is a great region to roam in. If that is lost to them, they are less than elk.

The American elk is a true stag, and many people think it should be called the wapiti, which is its Shawnee name. For the elk of the Old World is related to our moose, which makes for utter confusion. Early travelers told of the "Great Stag that was of the bignesse of a Horse," and its present name was first used when Captain Weymouth, in 1605, wrote his *Voyage to Virginia*: "Some like our other Beasts, the Savages signe unto us, with horns and broad ears, which we take to be Olkes or Loshes."

It is estimated that at one time there were probably over ten million elk in North America. They ranged over the greater part of the continent, from Massachusetts to British Columbia, from Texas to Great Slave Lake; and as late as 1826 there were still herds in Pennsylvania.

But our record for destroying these great herds is as shameful as our massacre of the buffalo. They could be hunted on horseback and were easily killed. Many thousands were slaughtered, often not for meat or skins, but simply for the sport or for the two rudimentary tusks which the elk alone have, of all the deer family, and which are prized as ornaments.

Now their wild range is limited to a few Rocky Mountain areas, the Olympic Mountains, and a strip through Manitoba and Saskatchewan. And even here they are on trial, for the farmers resent them if they increase in numbers and spread down into the plains. The fall after we were there two thousand of the animals suddenly got the gypsy urge and started off across the farming country, eating late crops, hay-stacks, and whatever else was in their path.

These gregarious animals travel in herds. They are said to be the most polygamous of the deer family, and in the fall the bulls fight fiercely for their harems.

Seton in *The Lives of Game Animals* tells of the strange circle dance of the elk, of which I had never heard and which appeals to my imagin-ation as did the elephant dance in *The Jungle Book*. In this dance the elk are said to move rapidly in a small circle, clockwise, with their noses close to the ground. In such a merry-go-round, the motion is a trot with occasional plunges into a gallop, and they stir up great clouds of dust which can be seen for miles. This seems an obscure ritual, having no connection with courtship or rivalry.

It was a great delight to pass these proud creatures. The late sun-light kept touching their spirited heads, their just-budded horns which would soon be the great symmetrically branched antlers. When their grave eyes rested on us as they turned, I felt exalted in their presence.

As the sunset threw its last gold splinters across the dim road we saw a big bull on a hilltop against a windy sky of orange and green with burned trees behind him. Lee had always wanted to see a big game

animal silhouetted on a skyline, and here he was, short and strong in the body, with powerful neck and legs and a most noble head.

That was a glorious picture. So was Moon Lake, with its pale shimmer broken only by a beaver swimming along the shore, while over the muskeg a golden eagle slashed through wild clouds of saffron and maroon.

Then the dusk deepened. Owls were calling. Peter saw three moose at the edge of a bog—a cow and two half-grown calves. They stood and stared at us in a vacant way before they ambled off into the alder bushes. It was exciting to have a glimpse of moose again, but after the distinction of the elk I must say they looked like three clodhoppers from the sticks, as of course they were.

When we left the park we had seen over sixty elk instead of the one I had hoped for, and I was too gratified to mind that the hotel had no dining room and that pitchers took the place of running water.

Next day rain was on the road ahead of us. But our zeal was not dampened and it was still early morning when we arrived at the park. The forest when we entered it was dark and dripping with raindrops. We thought we might not see any game this chilly day—a tragic idea, for both Lee and Peter wanted action sketches of the elk.

I think it had disappointed the men at Delta because Lee had not made more sketches of the ducks. But he knew ducks so well that it wasn't necessary—just to see them was enough to refresh and revise his knowledge. (Ruddies, however, he had never known, and he did make sketches of them.) He had never in his life had such a chance as this for detailed study of elk—if only they had not vanished into secret shelter!

Peter was again the first to spot a game animal—he certainly had an eagle eye! A young moose was halfway up a steep hill, in among brown branches, and even when you knew it was there, it required the utmost strength of will to see it.

Soon we began to come upon the elk. Five bulls were in pale grass; against the dark sky, in the mist and the rain, they were superb. When one caught sight of us he drew his head back in a slow arch with his nose raised, and the sweeping gesture was one of the most beautiful I have ever seen. In that movement he resumed his lost sovereignty.

Down the slope more were feeding. Elk eat grass and weeds, shrubs, and deciduous trees as well; in winter they live on the roughest food. Lee noticed that the young bulls did not seem to have dropped their spike horns; all the does looked quite small, and we wondered if the older females had already withdrawn so that their calves could be born in solitude.

Two of the bulls were couched on a hilltop screened by purple birch twigs with freshfallen snow around them. They rose as we stopped the car. Lee and Pete began making quick sketches of their various poses, exclaiming over the beauty of each powerful motion and talking eagerly of going on an elk hunt in the fall.

I knew these plans were daydreams. I knew too that man's urge to hunt is as deep in his blood as the elks' urge to roam. But that understanding was in my mind; emotionally, I was horrified.

"Men!" I said to myself. "Here are Pete and Lee, intelligent and kindhearted, crazy about the life in these creatures, and at the same minute panting to kill them. I can never grasp that it is an actual fact that each man kills the thing he loves."

"Each *one* kills the thing he loves," myself corrected. "You have the profoundest convictions about wildflower conservation, don't you, and you know perfectly well how the fresh beauty goes the minute a stem is broken, and that wildflowers are all wrong indoors anyway, and yet you can't help picking them in spite of yourself, now and then. You *have* to do something about their appeal and what you do is destroy it. What about those Canadian violets?"

"Why are you looking so guilty?" Lee asked. I can't even think without being found out—I have to lead the most exemplary life!

Now our rain-swept road woke up. First an elk was lying in it, for some unaccountable reason. He jumped up, cow-fashion but more

swiftly, and leaped in alarm to the edge of the wood, where he hesitated with his absurd stub of a tail, so unsuited to the dignity of the animal, stuck straight out. Next, a black stump in the road turned out to be a bear, who ran with singular speed into a thicket and looked out at us with vicious little eyes. He really had a baleful look, as a bear should have; Peter was very pleased with him.

Whitethroats were calling their *sweet—sweet—Canada—Canada* in the rain, and I thought that the song would always mean a Manitoba spring to me, wherever I might hear it after this.

In a dark pool surrounded by dripping pine boughs, a mallard pair was swimming contentedly side by side, with the raindrops making silver splashes all around them on the black surface of the water. We passed more and more elk, and watched to see them raise their heads, arching their necks in that regal and unforgettable gesture, before they vanished into the mist.

We were on another planet from the sunny one we had known at Delta. This was a shadowed world, with ancient nobility under its drooped branches—there was an unfathomable value in the companionship of these dispossessed, who had once had a continent for their estate. When we came upon a great herd, more than a hundred, in a forest of small aspens, and they vanished through the gray trees, they were a glimpse from a lost age, a sight to dream of.

If we could only hear their autumn bugling, we said, that "tremendous guttural roaring that rises in pitch to trumpet tones, higher and higher, till it breaks into a shrill screaming whistle"—what a sound to hear through these hills on a moonlit night!

The rain began to change to snow, the elk disappeared, and we gave up going across the mountain again. We had a wild blizzard on the way home, a blinding storm of snow and sleet that swept horizontally across the plain. All the Canadian air had gone down south to the States. This was Siberian.

In the midst of this snowstorm we saw the saskatoon flowering for the first time, its clusters of narrow white petals making the bushes look like airy snowdrifts along the road. It was a welcome reminder that the season was spring, whatever the weather. We were to meet this flower all over western Canada; plain or mountain, it made no difference to the saskatoon.

By the time we reached home, the north was clear, but over the ridge the sky looked black and the spring trees stood out in a curious bright copper color against the dark storm. Scores of hermit thrushes, usually so solitary and withdrawn, were flitting about the ridge in flocks, though they were too cold to sing.

At night, there was a wonderful moonlit sky littered with big fast-flying clouds, star-decorated. I never saw transparent clouds decked out in stars before. It was too exciting a night to stay indoors, so Grace, Lyle, Lee, and I drove out to see the marsh and the deer by moonlight. Then we came back to their ex-mink-house for a midnight candlelight supper of lobster salad and coffee.

Later the clouds swept down again and the north wind rose in strength. Our tiny house fluttered like a poplar leaf all night long. I liked the feeling of the great isolated country outside, the sound of the water which stretched north into arctic tundra, and the shaky comfort of what the Canadians always called our "little wee caboose."

6.

Across the Prairie Provinces

WHEN we left Delta, one morning in the middle of May, it was still cold and raw; in fact, we found ice in our water barrel. I had been afraid, the night before, when we had a chilly farewell picnic in the Hochbaum garden and the sky cleared reluctantly in the north, that the next morning might tempt us to take to the canoe instead of to the car. But it remained satisfactorily dour, and though we left with regret, we knew we would see our Deltonians again in June on our way home.

Our friends, both Canadians and Americans, had pitied us for having to make the long drive of a thousand miles across the prairies of Manitoba, Saskatchewan, and Alberta. Of course, they said, it would be wonderful in the mountains, but that long, long drag across the plains was such a bore.

A bore! We were sometimes tired, sleepy, thirsty, and dusty, but we were never bored for a single moment. The three days we spent crossing the immense prairie to the Rockies were among the most fascinating of our whole trip.

Of course it must be remembered that if Lee and I were as addicted

60

to drugs or drink as we are to country-crossing, we would be pronounced incurable. And then it was May and there was very little travel on the gravel roads, so that heat and dust were not annoyances as they might have been in midsummer.

So we reveled in these "lonely lands, ringed by the azure world." The monotonous flatness of the land seemed a transcendence; its emptiness was a delight.

In New York, I had become, after reading Korzybski's *Science and Sanity*, so conscious of the masses of words that were continually deluging us that I felt smothered as if in thick batter. I, whose favorite occupation had always been reading! But there was too much print, too many voices. We seemed to have less and less chance for tranquillity—dailies, weeklies, monthlies, books, radios, lectures shrieked and howled about the malevolence of the world, and tons of information, avalanches of advice, on every phase of life, poured in on us so fast that we had no way of finding out what was authentic and what false. I was suddenly overfed and nauseated with information.

Now we escaped words. We were starved, not surfeited. We now had time for knowledge. Very simple knowledge, to be sure, just the sights and sounds of a Canadian prairie in the spring, but the very simplicity of the lore was invigorating. There was time for its consideration—even, I thought, there might be a chance to garner a grain or two of that lovely and half-forgotten thing: wisdom.

It was a keen refreshment to realize our planet, not as the world but as *the earth*. I had never before had the feeling so strongly that I could experience the round globe—our earth itself, on whose thin crust we spend our chance hour. I had noticed the curvature of the earth at odd times, but here I could see it continually, in all directions, so that I coud *feel* that our sphere floated in the universe. Primitive awe took possession of me.

Traveling through Manitoba, we were first in familiar farmland. At Carberry, where Ernest Seton Thompson lived as a boy, we took a side trip into the Spruce Forest Reserve. This was a unique region where great sand dunes were covered with pale grass, through which were scattered, singly, tall wide-branched spruce trees. This was the setting of Seton's famous *Trail of the Sandhill Stag*.

West of the sand-hill country, we really entered the far west. As the day cleared, the Canadian air was deliciously crisp and tart. The land became more rolling, the brown grass had the faintest glint of spring, and there were ragged clumps of trees. Now and then large comfortable barns stood above meager houses.

As we drove west the fields expanded to enormous areas. I had always loved our own western wheat fields in midsummer, but those rich yellow seas never impressed me more than these empty spaces across which unbelievable multitudes of green barbs were just visible —tips of green spears "pricking on the plaine," wheeling as our car moved past, as if myriads of gentle knights were galloping in close ranks just underneath the surface.

These plants, and later the prairie grasses, making their steadfast march across the interminable miles, were impressive because of their very fragility. As the small stems of grasses sweep across earth horizons, their creative power has a curious impact on mankind, an enchantment which we do not consciously realize.

They have an incalculable strength. Grasses are the greatest lifters of water in all vegetation; the tiny root hairs, which collect the moisture, shower out from the base of the plant till their lengths reach unbelievable totals. The myriad roots of one plant of winter rye, measured scientifically, had a combined length of six thousand miles! And as we see their narrow blades reaching upward, we feel intuitively that all living things depend upon a leaf. Since the creation of food by the sunlight's energy can take place only through the leaf's surface, these wild grasses, these cultivated grains, are infinitely dramatic.

Canada's wheat lives on soil which is the country's most permanent natural resource, and southern Manitoba, Saskatchewan, and Alberta contain more than half of the total arable land in the Dominion. The soil has a marvelous fertility, there is "no speck of grit in it." It is a rich accumulation of plant life, layer after layer manufactured through the ages in long summer days, laid down in the autumn, and protected by the very intensity of the winter's cold, which preserves the plant food.

The soil has been accumulating ever since the Ice Age, and the land is not so eroded as our own plains are. For the level earth lies on horizontal shales which were formed before the glacial periods, and only occasionally do you find deep valleys. In some of these, cut below the deep soil into the soft rock by the streams of earlier times, the rivers still flow; in others the water has disappeared as the climate has grown drier. There are few streams, for evaporation equals the rainfall in many places, and the surface water usually collects in shallow lakes, ponds, and potholes, with no outlets.

Sometimes the land is parched with drought; in this most prosperous farm region of the whole world people have been close to starvation. Often as we drove along we saw deserted farmhouses leaning crazily to one side as their log foundations rotted away. In a mere forty years this prairie was settled, had a tremendous success, and went down to destitution in a remarkably swift cycle.

And I don't know of any more hairbreadth escape than wheat had when the early variety first entered this country. When wheat crops were first planted here they did not succeed, as the dry plains needed desert plants and the early frosts made quick-maturing a necessity. But there happened to be in Ontario a Scotch farmer, David Fife, who liked to experiment with seeds.

In 1843 he asked a friend to send him various samples of wheat from England. He received a quart or two of grain which had originated in Danzig, Germany, but almost all of this turned out to be winter wheat. Only a few kernels were typical spring wheat, and three of these seeds were adapted to the climate and sprouted. Of these three sprouts, one was eaten by a cow; the other two survived, and matured ten days earlier than any other wheat.

Fife succeeded in gathering a store of this precious grain, which he called Red Fife, and that was the beginning of the mighty Canadian wheat crop. Later, at the Central Experimental Farm in Ottawa, this grain was crossed with a variety from India, and the result was Marquis wheat, which matured six to ten days earlier than the Fife and had a greater resistance to rust. "Its introduction into Canadian agriculture," says L. H. Newman, the Dominion cerealist, "completely overshadows in importance any other single event, marking as it does a new epoch in the agricultural and industrial life of Canada."

But Marquis was susceptible, to some extent, to the dreaded wheat stem rust, which is a fungus growth that utilizes food needed by the wheat in order to develop its grains. The worst epidemic of this rust was in 1935; thousands of acres of wheat were never harvested. This was a tragic year, but it was also the year when several experimental wheats demonstrated the power to withstand attacks from rust. Now Marquis wheat has been superseded by varieties derived from it, which mature even earlier, resist rust, and give heavier yields. Governmental scientists are still making improvements on these strains.

In the meantime farmers had undergone superlative ups and downs. At first there had seemed to be no limit to the wealth to be won by wheat raising. There was a great boom; half a billion dollars poured into the hands of less than ten million people. But then came nine years of drought, rust, and grasshoppers.

Land that was too arid for farming had been plowed, and it simply blew away. The world did not want wheat, and crops piled up unsold. When the war began many markets were closed and the farmers were forced to live on relief. Yet they continued to grow wheat.

Now, this spring, with the great world need for food, the largest crops ever sown were being planted. It was an exciting and inspiring

thing to see this beginning of green life which would help to save humanity all over the globe.

As we came closer to Manitoba's western border, alkali began to show in patches of white along the road. I had thought crossing the border into Saskatchewan would be like entering Islandia or Graustark; the province had always seemed an imaginary land to me.

But now it was New York and not Saskatchewan that seemed a faraway legendary place. It is as John Burroughs wrote in his journal, "the universe, eternity, the infinite are typified by the sphere. . . . We speak of the ends of the earth, but the earth has no ends. On a sphere every point is a center and every point is the highest point, and this explains the puzzle of time and space. . . . This moment is the center of Time; this instant is the highest point in the revolving sphere."

Over the snowy drifts of the saskatoon flew mountain bluebirds, with backs and wings of glittering sapphire and breasts a softer blue. Taverner in his *Birds of Western Canada* says, "A famous writer has described the eastern bluebird as 'the sky above, the earth beneath,' referring to the blue back and red breast. Following this figure of speech, the mountain bluebird is purely celestial, with no earthly

contamination." We also saw a hawk new to us, the Swainson's, which is the common hawk of these prairie provinces. About the size of a redtail, it varies in plumage (this one happened to have a great deal of white) and resembles the black vulture in its flight.

The thickets of aspen, almost the only tree now, had become so small that, as Lee said, you could "almost plow 'em under." The roadside ditches were used as sunken roads by the occasional riders and horse-drawn vehicles. We passed Primrose Farm, and its name had a terrible pathos to me—I could imagine someone remembering English forests—but Lee said it was not necessarily a sorrowful name; perhaps it was the end of a primrose path!

In the immense circle of land, tiny details became important—the snow fences, the haystacks, the occasional windmills. Over the bleached stubble the men, the six-horse teams, and the tractors looked like the smallest toys, and a faroff train was too diminutive even to be played with.

The miniature elevators on the horizon showed where the invisible railroad tracks took their way. Elevators became most important on this endless surface. As we came toward a small town we could tell its size from far away by the number of grain elevators. A three-elevator town was likely to have a store or two and a handful of houses; a six-elevator town had a main street, with a collection of little shops along it, parallel to the railroad track.

"The inhabitant of the Prairie Provinces," Macintosh says in *Prairie Settlement*, "is peculiarly dependent on railways. . . . When the railway

66

passed a village by, the whole village, buildings as well as people, has frequently been moved across the prairie to the railway. The railway with its unfailing accompaniments, the loading platform, the two to five grain elevators, the post office, general store, machinery shed, and branch bank, closes the circuit through which the power of the world's economic organization flows into the pioneer community. What the birch canoe was to the fur trader, the railway is to the farmer of western Canada."

Lee was fascinated by the pictorial possibilities of the grain elevators. He could hardly pass by a town without taking a picture of them, and as it grew late in the afternoon and I longed to reach Regina, I really

hurt his feelings by failing to be enthusiastic over one more picture of stalwart elevators which looked, to my weary eyes, just like the previous twenty we had photographed.

We realized suddenly, as we drove along, that Saskatchewan had no billboards along its roads, and decided that it was the most intelligent of provinces.

Regina was a welcome sight when at last it came into view. It is the capital of Saskatchewan, a town of over fifty thousand population, and most impressive with its great stone Legislative Building enhanced by a blue lake with extensive gardens about it, a fine college, and a prosperous business district. The Royal Canadian Mounted Police, who have their western headquarters here, add color to the town literally and figuratively.

How I appreciated the big Canadian National Hotel! There is nothing like camping out, even in caboose comfort, to make one realize how luxurious a modern hotel really is, how marvelous the unlimited hot water, the soft beds, the electric light!

In the morning we woke to thunder and lightning, and at breakfast we heard the Canadians congratulating themselves on a ten million dollar rain; I overheard one man say, in cheery tones, that the crops in the States were suffering badly from both drought and insects.

When we started out, rain was still falling from the dark and heavy sky. But once on the road again, we found a line of pale light low in the south, and soon silvery clouds blew along the horizon toward which we headed.

We were in open grassland today. No more trees, except around farmhouses, every one of which we could count. Each isolated house and barn had a whole covy of stark little sheds between them, making every home into a tiny village. In this country, the telephone poles had great character: they strode in front of us until they dwindled into the distance, looking as close together as if they were leafless groves.

The sun was bright by the time we came to Moose Jaw. Moose Jaw surprised me, for the name had made me expect one of the more dejected western towns. Not at all; it was a cheerful place with trees along its paved streets and buildings bright and glittering in the smokeless air. It even had a Scottish Curling Club.

West of Moose Jaw, we came to hills.

Now the whole great plain in Canada slopes down from the foothills of the Rockies to the east and north. There are three distinct levels. At Delta we had lived on the lowest, eight hundred feet above sea level, on the "black earth" soil which was the Agassiz lake bed. The western boundary of this is the Manitoba escarpment, of which Riding Mountain is a part. West of this, the second prairie level, the "brown soil," is a rolling plateau with an altitude of about sixteen hundred feet. That level we had been riding across; and now we came to its boundary, where the ridge of hills rises three hundred to five hundred feet, after which the third prairie level slopes to the Rockies, from two thousand two hundred to four thousand feet at the foothills.

We celebrated our arrival at the third level by exploring on foot. The Indians drive their wagons along the wide ditches which run parallel to the graveled roads; we walked down one ditch, then crawled under a barbed wire fence and up across a hilltop. As the sun rose higher, so did my spirits. The sky had water-color clouds put in with

no hard edges, the grassy hills were now silver-pale and now swept with purple shadows that looked solid enough to be runaway islands.

The May wind shook out the flowers of the golden pea, creamy birdfoot, and wild candytuft. We heard a horned lark sing, and in a pasque flower cup I found a small bee curled, fast asleep. During working hours too. I was pleased to find one bee not virtuously busy, and I hoped he would not be found out. He looked as irreproachable as a baby asleep with its fists above its head. In such spacious landscapes,

any bit of life makes a profound impression, and I remember that bee as vividly as I do the Riding Mountain elk or the Delta swans.

"There's a haw—caw, caw, caw!" said Lee, as a crow flew off a fencepost.

I laughed as derisively as the crow. "You thought it was a hawk, you know you did!" I said. "You needn't try to crawl out like that. Shame on you, are you an ornithologist or a mouse? Just admit the crow fooled you!"

"For anybody who makes that mistake about once a week, you're crowing a lot," Lee protested. "For anybody who announced in public that she couldn't identify crows!"

"And I never wrote anything that brought such friendly responses," I said cheerfully. "Strong silent men broke down and spent pages in confessing they have never been sure of crows either. I made people feel they were not alone in their shame. I shed rays of sunlight on the secret guilt that they felt when crows kept fooling them. I—"

"Why do you blame everything on the crow?" Lee asked. "If I may be so bold, isn't there some lack in the party of the second part?"

"I know it's the crow," I answered positively. "You never mistake another bird for a crow, do you? It's always the crow who deceives you into thinking he's something else. That proves it's completely deliberate."

Magpies were everywhere. Magpies are the only birds I invariably think of as feminine; as they sweep by in striking black and white, with long trains and great white fans for wings, they seem beautiful and wicked sirens. They prey not only on the eggs and young of other birds, but on sheep and cattle; they have the sickening habit of tearing at any sore or insect bite on an animal till they often inflict fatal injury.

Ground squirrels were all over the road. These were not the Franklin which we had seen at Delta, but Richardson ground squirrels that like the open plains and are never found in brush or woods. They are called flickertails from their habit of raising the end of their tails as they whistle. They are supposed to stay in the neighborhood of their burrows all their lives, hardly going more than fifty yards from the door, but these were not such stay-at-homes; they went skittering across the highway far ahead at lightning speed, like distraught dots and commas.

We came to a region of virgin prairie, and drove for many miles through desolate and uneven hills with hardly a sign of human existence except our single line of road. At long intervals a house standing against the level skyline made me think of *Through Dry Plains*.

Under the great evening sky,
Across the wide semicircle of dim land,
Small and desolate, here and there are homesteads.

Tiny, alone and valiant. Each astrain
With misery or delight, inch-high they stand
In the indifference of the darkening earth,
Under the clear peace of infinity.

The landscape needed buffalo to complete it. Instead we saw our first cowboy who—O tempora, O shade of The Virginian!—was driving cattle with a tractor.

The storm clouds became menacing. The feeling of being penned in by ominous hills was suddenly disquieting after our horizontal freedom. In a wan light the clouds ran in black tumbles above the lonely skylines.

"Uninhibited, uninhabited," I murmured.

"Unrabbited, I'd say," Lee returned. "We haven't seen a jack rabbit since we started. Or any grouse, for that matter. This must be the lowest ebb in their cycle of abundance and depletion."

At Chaplin we turned off our gravel road, the principal highway across Canada, and walked down a rutted lane to see Chaplin Lake. This stretch of alkaline water was so pale that the navy-blue hills, in shadow behind it, were startling in their intense color. (Alkali is a mixture of mineral salts which include limestone, gypsum, Epsom salts, common salt, and potash. The soluble salts are leached from the soil

73

by drainage and concentrate in solid white beds, sometimes forming layers which are many feet in thickness.)

The surrounding prairie sloped down very slightly to the expanse of chalky white with faint watery streaks of gray. The whole lake was almost dry, almost dead, and I had never seen a lake dying—I did not like it. Even the little water which remained had no ripples in it in spite of the strong wind. It lay thick and torpid and spent. A willet was walking in this water and his footprints remained stamped in the liquid behind him.

In the early afternoon we came to what had been Rush Lake, once a marshy body of water famous as a wildfowl breeding ground. Now it was only a depression with dead rushes standing in it. "This is a much more pathetic sight than your Lake Chaplin," Lee said. "This lake was man-murdered."

Rush Creek, a little farther on, had not been drained, however; it still had water flowing. Here we found a strange situation. The stream was canopied with flashing wings. Thousands upon thousands of Franklin's gulls were tilting above it, crowding each other in the air; and up and down its narrow channels they swam in a milling mass. With their little black caps and shrill short cries they seemed like swarms of children just let out at recess time. Lee thought these great numbers had probably nested in Rush Lake in former years and now that the lake was gone they came back to the nearest water, however inadequate that was.

As the birds flew above the curves of the creek, the rosy flush on the myriad breasts and necks was very evident. Lee had seen these lovely birds in Chile and Peru, for they winter in South America, some of them even flying down into Patagonia. In North America they stay on the inland prairies; we had seen them in South Dakota and Montana in great flocks, but never in such a concentration as we watched here.

We came to our first sagebrush, looking dull green from the car, but it was lovely silvery stuff when I picked it. After the scent of pine, the smell of sagebrush comes next on my list of favorites.

There were other alkali lakes, but not dead ones; they had pale water, gray-green and dim blue, and ducks swam in them. I wondered about the Epsom salts in the water. One pond had several hundred of the dainty phalaropes, spinning round and round like aquatic tops. These were northern phalaropes, even smaller than the ones we'd seen at Delta. Avocets were about, and curlew.

I had a nap and awoke choked with dust. The distance was gray with it, and dust whirlwinds ran all over the landscape, as we came to plowed land again. We saw these dwarf cyclones for many miles, wavering across the fields like the ropes of India's magicians standing without visible support. One, swooping down a slope with a long trail of dust after it, seemed an unusually emaciated dragon with its hungry head reared high in the air. It slithered down a hill after a six-horse plow, missed it, veered across the road ahead of us, and moved more slowly up another slope.

There was more and more dust, and we were choked with thirst. Stones hit the car floor with a sharp clatter, the road grew rougher by the minute, and I felt I could not stand one extra jolt without falling into bits like a disrupted jigsaw puzzle.

I spoke sharply to myself. Riding in supercomfort on a graded road with a hotel (I hoped) ahead of me, what had I to complain of? Think of the early travelers, I told myself, the ones who, in the late seventies and early eighties, sent back reports to would-be settlers. (For the settlement of western Canada began only after 1870, when the Canadian government decided the agricultural possibilities of the country were too favorable to allow the fur trade to monopolize it, as it had until that time; and rapid settlement began only after 1900.)

These first travelers drove mules thirty or forty miles a day, if luck was with them; if not, they forded streams and waded in mire, their wagon wheels sinking to the axles in mudholes, with mosquitoes

75

and flies "vicious and numerous." "The truth is," one wrote, "there are *no* roads in the country. A road originally consisted of two rut-marks on the prairie sod . . . on the main trail twenty such ruts can now be counted running parallel. Outside of Manitoba no attempt whatever has been made to either bridge a creek or drain a slough and each traveler does the best he can."

Prairie fires traveled as fast as a galloping horse, and sometimes ran unchecked for a hundred miles. The bones of slaughtered bison lay around campsites. Wolves could be seen dodging around the willow thickets. Wigwams might suddenly spring up like mushrooms, and then the Indians danced and yelled all night to the "hum-drum of the tom-tom." "The result was," the narrator adds piteously, "we had little or no sleep and felt indisposed the next morning." There was little water. "A half breed's plan of getting good water," another writer says, "is to taste it, and if it is no worse than a weak infusion of Epsom salts, he will pronounce it very good for tea."

But in spite of comparing such hardships with my fortunate state, the rolling prairie had rolled long enough for me. I was looking eagerly for Maple Creek, where we had to stop no matter what it was like.

7. Antelope Country

Maple Creek was a good little town. It actually had a creek. It had trees, and lilacs in bloom. The country hotel was a haven of rest; our room was enormous, with a closet as big as our caboose had been. After supper we took a walk along a country road with mallards flying in courtship flights along the creek; I could feel myself still joggling from the long ride over gravel, as you feel a ship's motion after you reach land.

Our destination was Banff and Lake Louise, but on our way we meant to stop over at Brooks, Alberta, in the heart of the antelope country. However, when the new morning was The Queen of the May, we decided to drive twenty miles out of our way, south of Maple Creek, to see Cypress Hills Provincial Park.

The meadow larks were shouting unrestrainedly as we left Maple Creek, and I couldn't blame them. Out of the sky of clearest turquoise came a west wind wild and sweet. The creek was choked with rapture, rosy maple flowers and pale-green willow leaves. Ancient cottonwoods were actually throwing shadows across our road. Imagine a *shadowy* road in Saskatchewan!

South of Maple Creek the level land began to billow up into wide knolls and grassy slopes, with the Cypress Hills ahead of us almost a table mountain, forested only at the top. In the light of early

77

morning, the great curves of silvery green had an incredible purity.

A stream cut down from the highlands, and stately cottonwoods stood in the shelter of its banks. Clean domes swept off from it, subtly contoured. Magpies flashed about in the gold sun that slanted down the hillsides. The whole landscape had a translucent look, as if it had been made from light, and I felt clarified by the fresh wind, scented with silvery sagebrush, which came by us in light swirls. I wanted to sing aloud, which is always a sign I am above myself. This was another of my "special moments."

Suddenly, up from a hidden ravine and across the road in front of us, flashed five antelope. I had not dreamed of seeing them this morning—antelope were to be near Brooks. I could hardly believe they were happening.

Tan and white, short, and strongly muscled, across the road they sped, and we felt our throats tighten as we waited to see them soar over barbed-wire fence to the open prairie. The expected leaps did not occur. With no lessening of speed they flashed *under* the lowest strand of wire, ran down a gully and up again, with white rumps fluffed out into rosettes, and stopped on the hill to look, pacing lightly and smoothly as they slowed down.

How did they get under that fence? It is still a mystery to us. If only we had not been so startled we might have seen what happened. They could not have stretched their forelegs out in front of them; but equally they could not have gone down on their knees.

Later we asked Carl Rungius, America's foremost painter of big game, and he could not explain it. He said that antelope were running, not leaping animals, and he had seen them run so low that they were almost hidden by sagebrush, but he did not know how they slid under that wire. He told us, however, that when the barbed-wire fences were new in the country, great numbers of antelope were killed by running into the strands. They would be piled along a fence. But now they have certainly conquered its hazard.

These pronghorns once ran in millions on the western plains. They are not true antelope; they are in a family all their own, though they copy characteristics of many animals—deer, true antelope, and cattle. They have a high sensitivity and do not live long when they are captive, even if the enclosure is a very large one. They must have the free sweep of open country.

In winter the whole herd seeks shelter in valleys or wooded regions. When spring comes the mothers go off to bear their young, and then the herd seeks the open plains. Through the summer the bucks live apart, but in the fall they join the herd, and as the rutting season approaches they become very active, running for miles at great speed.

In the fall each buck tries to collect as many does as possible, and becomes very pugnacious. When a buck fights he can inflict great injury with his horns, the inturned points of which may catch in the throat of a rival, ripping it open. The prongs may also serve as a guard, and prevent a thrust from another buck from slipping down the horn and reaching the head.

After our five antelope vanished, we went on into Cypress Hills Park, which has the highest elevation in the province, forty-three hundred feet, which is the same elevation that Banff has. The high weathered hills, plateaus, and deep ravines have, the guidebook says, been compared to the Scottish Highlands. They were battlegrounds of the Blackfeet and the Cree, as Riding Mountain was.

The dense forest here is of spruce and lodgepole pine, and is the most easterly point reached by the lodgepole. It was a most abrupt change from the short-grass plains surrounding it, and it seemed delightful, as we walked through its cool shadows, to hear the breeze tangling in the pine tops, after the unimpeded prairie wind. Terns flashed over its dark lake and above the summits of the hills, where an eagle should have been, soared a great blue heron.

After we left the shadowy branches, the level country seemed emptier than ever. Yellow road scrapers were a large part of the scenery, and ground squirrels followed behind them as crows follow a plow. At noon we crossed the border of Alberta and reached Medicine Hat, a modern town delightfully situated on the Saskatchewan River at a junction of valleys.

We had lunch on a bluff which overlooked the river, and it was hard for me to believe I was actually sitting "by the banks of the Saskatchewan."

On toward Brooks, the country became almost desert, with little vegetation, and cactus mixed with the sagebrush. The sun was fogged with dusty gray, which made the sparse towns we passed look more dismal than ever. One had its forlorn houses scattered far apart, as if it were too much trouble to be neighborly; the spaces between were used for dump heaps. There had been no rain here for a long time.

But there was an excess of flickertails. The road margins were honeycombed with their burrows, and the little creatures galloped gaily

80

across our path, giving joyful leaps now and then, as the deer had at Delta. There were too many of these jaywalkers; we could not slow down for the hundreds of them, and I tried not to look back.

The paved road near Medicine Hat had been neatly carpeted with their carcasses. Now on less traveled roads, there were large family gatherings around each flattened relative. I thought they were mourning parties; Lee said they were cannibalistic feasts. He was right, I am sorry to say. Though much of their food consists of roots, leaves, and seeds, these Richardson ground squirrels are also carnivorous and Coues speaks of seeing them feasting on dead buffalo.

After a time we began to see antelope on these waterless plains. The small animals, a bold bright tan with accents of white and black, held their heads high; their ears were very mobile, and they had short manes which stood up in a spirited way. In fact the whole creature had a most distinguished and virile look.

Before we saw one large group with our field glasses they had caught sight of us, for their large lustrous eyes are reputed to have the keenest sight in the animal kingdom. They were alert and wary. But when the large buck decided we were harmless he lay down in the sagebrush and the others took to grazing, although they lifted their heads every few minutes to watch us.

These pronghorns eat grass, greasewood, and sagebrush. They also relish cactus, which seems an unappetizing choice until one understands that in arid regions they get their water as well as food from these prickly plants.

The more desolate the land became, the more antelope appeared. It was an extraordinarily heartening and exciting thing to see. Here is one species which seems definitely on the way up instead of out.

In 1883, John Macoun (who called the pronghorn by the odd name of "Cabree"), stated that within the past few years the animals had nearly all been killed by the starving Indians. Although in 1879 there had been droves of ten to fifteen (just such herds as Lee and I had

been seeing) south of Battleford, those had nearly all disappeared by 1882. But in the just-published *Catalogue of Canadian Recent Mammals* R. M. Anderson records such an increase in numbers, owing to judicious protection, that in 1944 there were about thirty thousand in Alberta and a lesser number in Saskatchewan.

The running of the pronghorn was marvelous to see. They never bounded, but raced in great circles about us, leaving us and then curving back in a wide arc to see us again. They ran as straight as if they were sliding along a wire. Only when they slowed to a trot did they have the slightest up-and-down motion; this trot was quite ele-

gant, with the graceful head lifted high. When they walked their steps were stilted, as if it were foreign to their natures to move so slowly.

One buck ran at full speed to an irrigation ditch, and in spite of the morning's experience we expected him to sail blithely over it. But he stopped to look at it with care, then made a clumsy little hop across it. We were told later that the pronghorns may leap into the air at times, but this is invariably a "spy jump" to see what the enemy is about.

When the animals are alarmed they run in a crowd close to the ground, so lightly and swiftly that their legs seem to blur into mist. Unluckily, their curiosity is as strong a characteristic as their watchfulness, and they can often be tolled within gunshot by a waving or moving object. Lee's father once used a buffalo skull to toll them in.

Our band ran for a long time in wide circles, and their white rump patches were conspicuous. Then, when the animals turned to face us, the whole herd seemed to disappear, blending into the landscape. The rump patches differ from those of the elk or other animals, and are most important to the antelope. As warnings of danger, they flash out as vividly as illuminated signs. The white hairs are short in the center of each patch and longer as they radiate outward, and a circular muscle running under the skin connects the roots so that the pronghorn is able, when it is alarmed, to flare the patches out into big white pompoms. At the same time, musk glands which are situated in the center of each of the rump patches send forth a strong odor which is an added warning to the herd.

The antelope's horns are also distinctive. Almost heart-shaped, pointed and curving inward, with pronounced prongs, they are true horns, hollow as those of cattle are; unlike cattle, however, the antelope has the unique peculiarity of shedding the horn in the fall, leaving a bony core remaining on the skull. Until it was discovered that this stub was permanent, there was a great controversy as to whether the animal shed its horns or not.

The last stop we made to watch the antelope was a fortunate one. The landscape was seething with ground squirrels. The prairie seemed to quiver like the skin of some great beast. It was a moving sight, to make an understatement. The flickertails are fond of society when they rise from their six months' hibernation, and all the plain was polka-dotted with their burrows. Each hole had a pair of squirrels, and every pair seemed to have a large family. They all scurried and flickered and romped and wrestled and caressed each other in a riot of activity. It was as bad as Coney Island.

A big creature ran across our road and stopped by the ditch; it turned out to be a badger. I had never seen one before, and I was surprised at its size. It was enormous, as well it might be with its food frisking about over every inch of the ground for miles in all directions.

The badger is built in a strange fashion; he can lie as flat as if he had no bones at all, and this one looked like a wet bath rug as he lay by his burrow. He had been in the water and his gray coat was dripping and matted; his broad head, however, striped vertically in black and white, was dry and had a savage tigerish look.

I had vaguely thought of a badger as mild and retiring, but as a matter of fact he is a fierce old warrior who will die fighting to the last rather than surrender. His thick, loose hide protects him like armor, and he is so strong that if he gets braced in his burrow it is almost imposible to pull him out.

I noticed that his tunnel had dirt scattered out on every side till it measured perhaps ten feet across. The badger digs such a hole spirally with his forearms, which have extraordinary muscles, the evolution of which is still a puzzle to scientists. If he sleeps in his burrow he sometimes plugs it several feet below the surface of the earth—just locking the door before he retires.

This is not a permanent home, however, for the grown badger seems as much a nomad as the wolf, wandering in the same way over a large circle, seeking what he may devour. But he is a solitary nomad, never traveling with others of his kind except in the spring, when a few may be together.

Cecil Huff, of Glenwood, Minnesota, who has made an intensive study of the badger, told us that in looking for his prey the badger will often enlarge a gopher hole till he can get his nose into it. Then he expels the breath from his lungs and wedges his face tightly into the burrow. As he takes in a deep breath he can scent any unlucky ground squirrel who is in residence underground, and he can dig even faster than his small victim can.

Our friend by the roadside looked at us steadily before he departed. I was impressed, until as he turned to enter his burrow he lost his dignity. His slightly tilted nose dispelled the tiger look, and his silver hair, parted in the middle all the way down his spine, made him a comic figure.

As he vanished, I caught sight of two burrowing owls. I sprang out of the car, for I had been looking for these little owls all across the provinces. They stood back to back on the strong yellow legs that looked too sturdy for the light weight of the bodies, and now and then they made little bobbing bows. As I moved closer, one disappeared down the burrow. I made my way slowly toward the other, playing "Stop" with it as we used to play the game at school, freezing when it looked my way, stepping forward when it twirled its head to look out over its back. I almost won. I almost touched it.

Lee had crossed the railroad track to walk along the irrigation ditch. As he was returning he heard a faint peeping, and down from the track marched two diminutive pintail ducklings, all alone. They had been swimming down the ditch and when the water was piped under the railroad, they simply walked up over the rails and down to meet it on the other side. Independent and composed, they took to the water again as Lee watched them. He called me over in time to see the black dots swimming intrepidly down their watery path.

"But look what I've found," I told him. "Come back on my side." Up from a gopher hole had reared a sinuous creature, far larger than I had known a weasel could be. It was the long-tailed weasel, which on the prairies seems to follow the Richardson ground squirrels wherever they go. It has no settled home and does not hibernate. Many animals, even when they do not sleep all winter, hole up in bad storms, but this bloodthirsty beast does not seem to be stopped by the wildest weather.

It was a fascinating, wicked-looking animal, dark on head and back, with a black tip to its long tail and a beautiful rich yellow on breast and legs. Its head was wide and flat and a black mask covered half its face, while the line between that and the yellow chin was curved in such a way as to give the weasel a smile, indescribably vicious and evil—far more startling than a ferocious expression.

It looked at us in a bold, reckless way, swaying its upper body in the air. Then as it slithered out of the hole and bounded lightly over the ground in long undulating curves, all the flickertails suddenly disappeared. It slid down into a burrow, and they all popped above ground and sat up in panic-stricken silence, with their hands clasped to their hearts.

I felt grateful that the baby ducks were far down the canal, headed away from such ferocity. More antelope ran across the horizon, and as Lee started the car a long-legged coyote sneaked through the fence and trotted off across the prairie looking over his shoulder at us.

"What a place!" I sighed with excitement. "Lee, I'm glad we decided to stay at Brooks a while. Think of seeing all those wild things in one stop."

"This is the first irrigation ditch," Lee said. "The animals must use it as a waterhole and congregate around it. Yes, we ought to see a lot in the next few days. Birds, too—there's a big waterfowl reservation south of Brooks with pelicans, geese, and shorebirds on it."

Little did we know, as the saying goes.

Brooks looked simply delightful from a distance. Long lines of cottonwoods and spruce were planted around the farmhouses; little fruit orchards, protected by hedges, were in bloom; there were spring gardens everywhere. After miles of sniffing desert dust, I was enchanted with the scent of apple trees and lilacs.

But in the town the streets were deeper in dust than the roads had been; we were smothered in it, and a dull haze of powdered earth hung in the air. The small hotel disappointed me by giving us a room with no bath attached. I felt gritty and neglected.

"Lee," I said, as he came in with more baggage, "are you *sure* they can't give us a room with bath?"

"Don't give it a thought," he answered cheerfully. "The city water system has broken down."

"It *can't*," I replied. Just then the housekeeper came hurrying by. "Shut the windows tight! Shut your car," she cried. "A terrible dust storm is on the way from Calgary."

"That's all we need," I said gently. We looked out. The sky in the west was black as carbon paper, with mustard yellow streaks flying ahead. Lee dashed down to close the car. The wind swooped and then the dust arrived.

It was like a sandstorm. Our closed windows might just as well have been open. Dust filled the room, our eyes and mouths were full of it. Outside the wind howled; black dirt swept around corners and blew from the roofs in great sheets, and in the dark blizzard men were the dimmest ghosts as they passed by. The papers said later that Calgary and other towns were completely blacked out by the dust, which rose in billows ten thousand feet in the air.

Then a wild rain stormed in. But it did not bring relief, it simply changed the dust into mud, while the wind reached seventy-two miles an hour and the temperature dropped thirty degrees in a few minutes. Cars in the street looked as if they had been stuccoed, their windows were thick with mud, their lights were blacked out, the horns too choked to blow. Even drivers familiar with the region lost their way on detours from Calgary; the buses could not get through. With a ridge of low black clouds running ahead of a mass of cold air and bringing gusty winds, rain, thunder, and lightning, it was the most spectacular line squall western Canada had seen in many years.

We went down to dinner to find the hotel jammed with most of the population of the countryside. People had come to town for some evening entertainment, and they all took refuge in the hotel. It seemed hours before we got into the dining room, and when we did the electric lights went off; we ate in a dense fog, with only lightning flashes to see the menu by.

The hotel staff was completely disorganized by such an unexpected mob, no water, masses of dust and mud, and a raging storm. They had more than they could manage, so the way they coped with one problem was simply to lock the rest rooms. When modern sanitation is erratic, the old-fashioned substitute ought to remain somewhere in the background. But Brooks was entirely up-to-date; even the station was locked, and we had no friends to consult. We drove out into the country.

But this was antelope country and had no bushes or bits of forest—only sheets of rain. And when Lee got out of the car his new hat blew off and scuttled down the road, hitting every puddle.

The next morning was rainy and very cold. Water remained A.W.O.L., and the hotel was too discouraged to serve breakfast. Lee and I looked at each other.

89

"I don't want to stay in Brooks," I said confidentially, looking out at the muddy streets and intermittent sidewalks.

"Let's go," said Lee, and soon we were far out along the drenched plains, on our way to Lethbridge and the Rockies.

8.

The Mountains' Edge

WE SET out very early from Lethbridge, in the chill of the dawn, to meet the mountains. The sky was overcast; but the air was buoyant and mild, the ponds full of ducks, and fenceposts tipped with. feathery gargoyles. However, as I had set my heart on first seeing the Canadian Rockies in the morning sun, truly the Shining Mountains, as the Indians called them, I was not appeased by lesser sights, however delightful.

We stopped at Cardston for hot coffee and a look at the Mormon Temple, impressive on a hill. After that, the flat land rolled into low grass hills, still a wintry brown. There were many sheep on this grassland, and behind them thunderstorms rollicked about the prairies. I counted six at one time, trailing black cloaks of rain around the vast horizons.

The car went down a hollow and came up over a slight rise into the middle of a herd of cattle. And there beyond the brown backs and the horns, where we took it for granted there would be only a bare plain, were magical apparitions. As suddenly as that, up out of the grass, a great procession of snow mountains stood before us.

All across the west they stood, and to the south of us they strode out into the plain. We had had no preparation whatever for them.

There were no foothills. Only brown grass and then these steep triangular escarpments, silver white, shadowed blue.

This was the Great Overthrust—occurring when lateral pressure pushed the ancient mountains for miles out over the young plain. There is no more dramatic sight in America and it seemed incredible luck that the clouds had lifted just at that particular moment.

As we drove west toward the Waterton Lakes, which are just north of our Glacier Park, every mile was more spectacular. "This is the greatest way to see the ranges," Lee said. "You *really* get them when you view them from the plains. You never see them from head to foot when you're in the midst of them."

The mountain masses were a deep plum blue with mantles of feather-white. Out of the narrow valleys at their feet, where the rustlers hid in the days of the great cattle ranches, swept billows of fog; and above their crags the storm clouds were lifting in great cumulus masses, bubbling high. The vertical battlements, jagged triangles, and violent thrusts of rock cut sharp against the sky were my childhood ideas of what mountains ought to be.

It was permissible to be overcome by their grandeur, for these mountains are carved from Pre-Cambrian rock, the oldest part of the world that our eyes can behold; the period of its formation is more than a billion years ago. Yet the mountains themselves are young things, geologically speaking, showing all the impetuous and headstrong characteristics of youth. Ranges rose up from an inland sea, were eroded, flattened, and lifted again. These present mountains arose, with infinite slowness, before the last Ice Age, when rock-slipping took place on a giant scale and the mighty Overthrust moved whole mountains, in the Glacier and Waterton Parks area, over the much newer prairie land to the east. The great isolated hulk of Chief Mountain is one remainder of this incredible action.

The granite core of the Rockies—the most ancient rock—is without layers. But over that were laid down thick beds of shales, sandstones, limestones—sediments from vanished seas. When these massive sediments were pushed aside, folded up, and twisted about, the granite core was thrust up from inside the earth.

As we approached Waterton Lakes Park we came to a rolling country of pale grasses. Here lay lower Waterton Lake, and as we entered the valley which had been hollowed out from the mountains' sides and made U-shaped by one of the many glaciers in ancient times, the upper lake gleamed between steep forested slopes, with the tiny village of Waterton Park on its shore. As it cut back into the mountains, the upper lake completely filled its narrow valley, while above it soared appalling pitches and exalted steeps. Their snows, we noticed, were oyster-white, because of those dust storms from Calgary which had blinded us at Brooks and which had billowed up even to the tips of these ranges.

After the endless expanses of dry plains, the liquid blueness of the lakes and the dark branches and scents of pine seemed almost unbelievable. And no sooner did we have shadows thick across our road than we began to see deer, all through the forest. Mule deer.

Now for many years our favorite animal in the Bronx Zoo was a mule deer. We had admired him intensely and longed to see such deer unconfined. It had been a disappointment not to see any on Riding Mountain; that disappointment was now more than canceled, for the stocky animals were everywhere about us, their lovely heads with the

94

big ears silhouetted against the sunlight. It was a marvel to see them.

In fact, there were more mule deer than people in the valley, for the tourist season, we thanked heaven, had not yet begun. The big chalet on a knoll overlooking the lake was not open, but we found a charming inn, Kilmorey Lodge, on the water's edge, where our windows looked out through pine branches to an emerald bay.

We stayed for more than a week there. The inn was run by Mrs. Reeves, whose mother had come to Pincher's Creek, the nearest railway station to the park, as a child of four, when it was a pioneer town and Indians were still somewhat of a menace. Most of the time we were the only guests.

Only once, on Queen Victoria's birthday, was the village crowded as it would be in midsummer; but even then the crowd was made up of neighbors: Blood Indians from Belly River, Mormons from Cardston, and the Hutterites who resemble our Mennonites but live in communal houses. I had hoped to see the Doukhobors, since they were a new sect to me. They are "spirit wrestlers" who left Russia to come here and wait for Christ's coming. They wrestle with demons and also with the police, for their way of protesting against earthly domination is to strip off their clothes and walk in solemn, naked procession. But the nearest lived some sixty miles from here and even they were not of the rebellious variety.

95

Except for that Victoria Day, we gloried in having the roads and trails to ourselves. Many of our naturalist friends scorn national parks as too civilized, while others think that they give one unparalleled opportunities for wildlife study. We join the latter group.

Of course the amount of civilization you find depends on the time of year. In the height of the summer season we ourselves would never choose the parks, for then the crowds take away what we are seeking, the companionship with wild creatures and the beauty of solitude. But early or late in the year, we escape the turmoil and see more wildlife by far than in sections which are hunted over. Of course nothing can equal a journey by pack train into the remote wilderness; however, when one is trying to get some comprehension of a quarter of a continent, national parks are the greatest boon, for there is easy access to exceptional beauty through the networks of trails and paths.

Naturally, as this was still May, many of the trails were closed. Our car could get only half way up Cameron Road, for it had had forty-five inches of snow two weeks before, and immense drifts blocked the last part of the path to Rowe Lake. Still, we were pioneers, of the year at least, and found an authentic tranquillity wherever we were able to wander. Besides, Waterton Lake was an appropriate place to linger, for it was named in honor of Charles Waterton, a naturalist and ornithologist who was one of the pioneers in conservation and founded one of the first bird sanctuaries in England.

On the first evening an exaggerated rosy glaze spreading across the snow above our pine-dark valley called us out-of-doors, and we walked down the road to Cameron Falls. The air raked cold and sweet across the spruce boughs, under which herds of mule deer were lying in gold-colored grass.

We came on three bucks grazing close to the road. They lifted their heads and then bounded off in the most extraordinary leaps, high in the air, not at all like the white-tailed deer.

"Look at them bounce!" I cried. "They bounce like tennis balls!
Look at *him*—he went up and came down in the same place."

"I've told you about that," Lee said in an accusing tone, amazed at
my amazement.

"But I had never realized they had such bounce. Why, they look
as if they were on yoyos!"

One buck was in the open, and I could see that he landed stiff-legged.
All four of his small hoofs hit the rock at the same time, making a
staccato rap each time he came down. There was hardly any movement
in his legs as he bounded; he seemed to rise from his toes. These deer
weren't trying to get away; when they really travel, they are said
to jump sometimes twenty or twenty-five feet at one bound. They
did not lift their black-tipped tails as they leaped—the under part

97

of the tail is bare, so they're sheepish about it. They do not have the white plume that the white-tailed deer is proud to display.

As Cameron Falls is unique in that its shelving rocks are tilted upward, its wild snow water had the sharpest tumult and all the showy white plumes that the mule deer lacked. Where the shining spray spread out into a dark and rocky stream, a water ouzel was balancing on a stone. We watched the little waterproofed bird walk into the stream and unconcernedly make his way up the rapids with his head under water, the waves glassing over his back. He looked so small it seemed impossible that he could make headway against such a violent rush of water, but he seemed to have far less difficulty than we do on Fifth Avenue.

Down the stream and *under* the low bridge flew a duck. Slate blue, reddish sides, spotted with white, edged with black—and it was following the curves of the stream, not cutting across them. "Was it a harlequin?" I cried incredulously. "I thought harlequins were arctic." Lee was excited too; the last harlequins he had seen had been in the Aleutians.

There were three more afloat in the clear lake, where remote summits were mirrored in the water in rose and dusky-blue. In beautiful plumage, almost as brilliant as wood-ducks, they were diving to feed and when they plunged up from under the lake, they rose with a plop that lifted them almost out of the water, as if they were little gas balloons. They bobbed upward as buoyantly as if someone had suddenly let go of a string which had been restraining them.

On the surface, their bodies rode high in the water. To dive they used their wiry tails as springs, and plunged under, where they swam with both wings and feet. These birds love swift water, and have been known to plunge blithely over waterfalls.

Along the shore, a grizzly came wandering out of the delicate green aspens. Gaunt and emaciated, he stood on his hind legs to see us as I raised my field glasses to look at him. He looked too big. "Let's get

98

back," I said urgently. "That black bear in Riding Mountain moved fast."

Later we met the De Vebers, who lived in a pleasant cottage across the road from Kilmorey Lodge and were most generous in their hospitality, and when we told Mr. De Veber, who is the Park's superintendent, about the bear, he asked us if we were sure it was a grizzly, as they do not come down to habitations as the black bears do. But our bear had the massive shoulders and the silvery overtones that are unmistakable and my theory is that he was still too drowsy from his long winter's nap to know just what he was doing.

Waterton appealed to us especially because here was the sharpest break between the mountain country and the plain. It was an added joy to wake up on a May morning to the singing of mountain birds and the scent of fresh snow, and then to drive out where green grass ran across the prairie land and the shallow ponds glittered with vigorous wildfowl. Or to have blue twilight fill our valley to the brim and then escape to the open plain which was still astir in the gold sunlight.

There were other edges too. There was the very edge of Canada; by one careless step we could fall off into the United States. A boat chugged down the lake past Hell Roaring Creek, so that one could see the Glacier Park range reflected in the water, and Goat Haunt Mountain, with no goats, alas, though their tracks were all across its snowbanks.

A magnificent road swung over Sofa Mountain, across the beautiful Belly River, and up again toward the boundary, the castellated peaks and diagonal soaring lusters of our own land. We felt a deep thrilling pride at the unfortified boundary line, clean cut through dense forest, going in peace up lonely mountains and down again. Thrilling too at the border's sign to departing guests: *Bon Voyage. Canada will always welcome you.*

Another edge was that between summer and winter; one only had to wander vertically. This made for a wide variety of flowery patterns. Waterton is famous for its floral wealth, and there were only a few steps to take from the earliest spring blossoms to midsummer ones.

In the flats by the river I found desert flowers in the hot sunny gravel. Ground daisies, pink and lavender with orange centers, or tiny pearl and rosy everlastings. And flat on the sand the entrancing velvet rosettes, circlets of bright yellow flowers surrounding centers of silver-gray foliage, so that it looked as if a great company had been recklessly casting down their golden crowns around the glassy creek.

Just a few inches higher on the meadow grass were mountain flowers: the alpine larkspur, short stemmed with large fire-blue blossoms, the yellow fritillary, grass orchis, and alpine phlox.

The outbursts of flowers came so suddenly! One day a hillside would be snow-sprinkled; the next, it was bright with the blooming balsam root, which had the look of spring sunflowers. In forest clearings whole meadows flamed out with the small shooting stars, vivid in the grass. These were cyclamens like our hothouse ones, but midget flowers, and far more wild and spirited. So spirited indeed that I could hardly believe the tilted petals did not have the power of flight. They seemed perched on their slender stems as if they had just alighted and might take wing again at any second, to fly in rosy swarms above the spruce tops.

Both by snowbanks and in among the pale green of the aspens the glacier lilies swayed in multitudes. Dogtooth violets, we call them, but here they were large and lilylike. I never felt the *activity* of flowers as intensely as I did this spring; the bud, the bloom, the seed—transformation came so swiftly. On the prairie the lilac petals of the pasque flowers, which look like giant anemones in their furry chalices, were already dropping, and above the green fingerlike leaves the plumes of smoky blue lifted in the wind. There were myriads of roseate plumes too, as the long-plumed avens changed from flower to seed. These were most curious plants, dyed with red from root to tip. The flowers looked like three large crimson buds dangling from three-branched stems of scarlet, for the pale pink petals were hidden inside a closed calyx.

Often as the color of these wildflowers was heightened by a spring rain, snowflakes would be falling on the pine needles just up the hill. Once I saw a rainbow bright against a snow flurry.

This was a bird edge too. The prairie ponds held many of the wildfowl we had seen at Delta, but the ducks at Waterton were species of the far northwest. The harlequins, particularly a pair which haunted our green bay, enchanted me, and for the first time I saw the Barrows, or Rocky Mountain, goldeneye. It differs from the American goldeneye, having a purplish head instead of a greenish one, and a crescent-shaped white spot on the face. In the mountains it sometimes nests as high as ten thousand feet, in hollow trees or in rock cavities. In its courtship it puffed out its iridescent head and took to solemn bowing, with sometimes an incongruous backward kick which sent a spray of water three or four feet in the air.

Then there was the lovely violet-green swallow, with subtle metallic plumage, which ranged up the mountains and into forests, but also flew with rapid wing strokes around the village docks. And we could hear it over the lake in the darkness before dawn. This flight song is part of the courtship; it is the only bird I ever heard of to serenade its beloved by late starlight. As the little troubadour sings, he flies, darting and twisting, around and around a small area, as if he were dancing to his accompaniment of song.

The mule deer, above all, are creatures of this edge country. When they run on level ground, they give an impression of great speed, but there they are not as swift as the white-tail. Their strategy, when in danger, is to head for broken country; in among rocks their leaping gives them a great advantage. Most people think that in these jumps they are traveling vertically rather than horizontally, but their flight is really astonishingly rapid for the terrain. They like the mountains' margins and they like forests, for they browse more than they graze. They are wanderers, far more than the white-tailed deer.

It was a delight to have these deer all around us. We never tired of watching them. To our surprise, our admiration was not wholly shared by the townsfolk. Looking at the beautiful heads and gentle expressions of these mule deer, it was hard to think of them as mischief-makers, but although they leave the valley as the tourists come in, they visit it by night, to ruin young vegetables and nip cherished roses as if they were so many Jack Frosts in buckskin. Mrs. De Veber spoke wistfully of finding every gladiola spray in her garden snapped off and then, to add insult to injury, left lying on the ground.

The road to Red Rock Canyon always had many deer, and it was our favorite drive. It ran along an old Indian trail by Blakiston Brook, with the Ruby Range to the south and Lone Mountain and Lost Mountain looming in the west. (There was Lonesome Lake too; someone had certainly chosen these names in a low-spirited mood.)

Waterton Lakes Park is noted for its rock color; the pyramided peaks and jagged ridges are streaked and barred with tawny orange and gold, pale green, purple and rust. But the deep ruby red on summits and on banded slopes is the richest coloring of all, and that is dominant along this valley.

The first evening that we took the ten-mile road we saw an elk on the skyline; and the mule deer were scattered on the slopes, with their long shadows trailing far downhill. I had counted sixty-nine on my side of the road, to Lee's sixty-four, when we saw our first mountain sheep and forgot to go on counting.

Six rams stood in dignified poses on a dark red outcrop, up a shale-sprinkled slope. I saw them first, but I couldn't believe it till Lee verified it; for I had expected, even if we were lucky enough to see mountain sheep, to spot them only as dots far up on a distant crag. These were only a few hundred feet above us.

I had not realized how distinguished and graceful these sheep would

be, with firm bodies, strong legs and rounded necks which held proudly the noble heads. The bold sweep of the horns fascinated me. It seemed strange that these mountain sheep were leaping animals, whereas the antelope were not; I had thought of them as heavy and unwieldy. But these rams, in spite of their thick tan coats (which are hairy and not woolly, although they are true sheep), looked active and muscular.

When they travel, they go in long single files, leaping up parapets, walking along dizzy edges, gazing down from domes of rock. Their feet have wide cushions of rubbery material which fit into crevices and grip a surface however slippery. As we gazed on these intrepid mountaineers I felt they were worth driving four thousand miles to see.

We spent one whole blissful day in Red Rock Canyon. In the early morning the sky was dark and there was fresh snow falling on the mountains. Over the windblown trees, a golden eagle flew. He was really golden looking; as a stray glint of sun illumined him, his wings, back, and head seemed spangled with gold.

All morning we studied mule deer, stopping every mile or so. It was wonderful to follow with our eyes the great sweeping lines that led from mountain top to valley and up again. In a beaver bog the clear water meticulously repeated the chickadees twirling in twisted poplars. The sun came out and we picnicked among spruces whose branches spread out like wide crinolines.

Above us a big ram lay on the edge of a parapet and looked down at us. We must have made him hungry too, for he walked with great dignity past the stunted timberline trees to graze on alpine flowers. These sheep seek higher and higher pastures as the summer progresses, liking especially the tiny secluded valleys between impregnable peaks.

After lunch we took a long walk up the Red Rock Canyon, which was a narrow chasm, a split in the mountain's side; its ledges were of deep red, the color of garnets, and so deeply scalloped that there were almost ruffles of stone. Emerald moss cushioned these ruby ledges, accentuating their color, and small spruces of vivid green were brilliant candelabra. Down at the bottom of the sundered rock where the snow water surged, the stony scallops were a luminous orange-red.

All around, the ranges stood high and white. Above the black shadows of the forest, the great hollowed-out cirques and amphitheatres were cased in snowy silver. To the southwest stood Mt. Blakiston, a gigantic tower crowned with the semblance of a ruined abbey, its gothic windows sheathed in ice.

A trail ran along the edge of the canyon, steeply winding through heavy thickets and tangled windfalls. Yellow violets glittered in the shadow, pine needles matted the path, and pine scent was buoyant in the air. I suddenly remembered the four grizzlies reported here last week and that only two of them had been killed, but I did not feel worried about them. It was the Rocky Mountain ticks I was really afraid of.

Although Waterton Lakes Park has fifteen hundred elk, we climbed to timberline without finding one, though there were many tracks. Down among the pines again in a moss-green hollow were sprays of bluebells which captivated me by being only two inches high. All through the trees they stood in delicate motion, their color an indescribably lovely shade between azure and hyacinth.

Lee began to sketch the pine trees and I lay down among the crowded bluebells. (I found them described in my wildflower book as lungworts, but I refuse to call them by that hideous name.) The sound of the Red Rock River was loud below us, the clouds went past faraway summits at a swift gallop, the sweet cool wind made me deliciously sleepy.

I was awakened by an eagle's scream. I sat bolt upright, to see two golden eagles, high above the forests, come together with outstretched talons. They grappled and fell through the airy heights, whirling round and round with their sweeping wings outspread, spinning down the blue abyss. They broke asunder, and immediately one was attacked by a Swainson's hawk, at which he turned completely upside down and slashed fiercely at the hawk, who ignominiously turned tail and fled.

Lee and I broke into exclamations of excitement. Lee thought one bird must have been defending his territory—a third eagle was also in the neighborhood—and I though it was a nuptial flight we saw, if by the word "flight" one can describe such wild tumbling.

I searched ornithological literature in vain for accounts of such activity and found nothing, except a description of the upside-down attack; I made fruitless enquiries. I found Roger Peterson had portrayed bald eagles in such a nuptial flight; that was something to go on.

At last George Sutton told me that he had recorded a similar incident in *Notes on the Birds of the Western Panhandle of Oklahoma* in the "Annals of the Carnegie Museum": "On September 29, 1933 . . . I witnessed a memorable aerial combat between two eagles that appeared to be tormenting and at the same time fighting over another eagle that was somewhat piebald in appearance and a little uncertain in flight. When I first saw these eagles all three of them were flying majestically toward a distant mesa. All at once two of the birds began diving fiercely at the other bird and this clumsy individual (perhaps a young one) made its way to the side of the mesa, where it hobbled about among the brush, dodging the repeated attacks of the birds in the air. Finally the two flying birds came to grips, grasped each other's feet with legs stretched far out, and whirled earthward in a series of breath-taking revolutions, catching themselves apparently just before they struck the rocks."

After our eagles disappeared we scrambled along a trail to Blakiston Falls, and it was late afternoon before we started back to Waterton. At that time hundreds of the mule deer were browsing in the meadows and through the aspen thickets in large herds.

They were in every mood that afternoon. Most of them did not mind our presence and we could study their handsome heads, the large gentle eyes, the dark patch on the forehead which adds such expression to their faces. Some of the bucks had horns almost half grown, others had only nubs. These deer had an extremely dignified walk, with their heads kept level and their legs held straight.

Many of the deer were curious about us and as they peered from shelter their large ears were sometimes held erect, close together, so that they looked like the ears of jack rabbits. Other herds were horrified at our appearance, and I was glad of that, for I loved to watch their high bounds, up over bushes, across tilted ledges, especially when a group of them went bounding like so many rubber toys. Sometimes a deer made a quick turn while he was still in the air, so he could see what we were up to, and would come down facing another way.

We found twenty-five in one tangle of brush and followed them across a meadow and up a steep cliff trail. They bounded away with that lovely *flying* look, and I surprised myself by chasing after them, shouting at their antic progress. It was the atmosphere of the Canadian Rockies that impelled me. The sparkles of the mountain air went to my head and made me feel a little intoxicated all the time.

9.

It Rained
in British Columbia

IT WAS time to be off to Banff, and the roundabout road seemed to us the most inviting. Lee decided not to drive north on the east side of the Rockies, but to cross Crowsnest Pass into British Columbia and see the long narrow waters of the Kootenay Lake country not far from the border.

Then we would drive to the north along the great Rocky Mountain Trench, a huge valley lying between the main Rockies and the older Selkirk ranges to the west. This U-shaped trough extends north and south through the whole length of British Columbia, and is one of the most remarkable topographic features in the western part of our continent. Farther north, we would recross the Rockies by the Vermilion Pass which leads east into the Lake Louise region. This was taking the three sides of an oblong, instead of driving in a straight line, but it was worth the extra mileage to us.

From Waterton Lakes we drove to Pincher's Creek through ranch and farm country and then turned west to the mountains again. After Lundbreck Falls, undulating hills, which looked as if they were covered with silvery green velvet, curved for long distances, their smoothness broken here and there by stone outcrops with wonderful old black pines or fresh green thickets crowning their rocky crests. Against these rugged islands saskatoon and white forget-me-nots broke in a surf of fragile mistiness.

We went from that into a coal mining district where the towns reminded me of West Virginia and Pennsylvania, with dingy houses all alike, bare yards, and side roads paved with slack. Each house had two bare poles for radio aerials. To add to the depression, a heavy blanket of clouds muffled the sky.

The desolation reached its climax at Frank, where the whole north face of the great Turtle Mountain had once slipped and crashed down to bury a little town. Though this took place forty-four years ago it is even now a stony desert. The debris still spreads like a fan across the valley. Boulders as large as houses fell with such terrific force that they extend high up the farther slope.

We came to a commemorative shield:

FRANK SLIDE

In 1903, April 29, 4:10 A.M., a gigantic wedge of limestone 1300 ft. high, 4000 ft. wide and 500 ft. thick dashed down and destroyed the town of Frank. Seventy million tons of rock swept over two miles of valley, taking 66 lives, burying numerous homes, the entire mining plant, railway sidings and 32,000 acres of fertile land to the depth of 100 ft., in approximately 100 seconds.

No wonder nothing has grown there since, if the stony debris is one hundred feet thick! It was a melancholy place on this gray morning and I was glad to get away.

At Crowsnest Pass the gnarled branches of pine and spruce leaned away from the prevailing wind which came through from the west. Crowsnest Lake was a dark greenish-blue, and the road ran through the pass with the tops of its rocky walls hidden in black clouds.

British Columbia greeted us in a growling, stormy fashion, as befitted such a mountainous province. But after we got through the pass

the storm changed to a gentle rain, and we noticed that on this side of the divide the tall trees stood perfectly straight instead of being twisted and windblown.

The country was the wildest we had seen; it seemed untouched by man. But although it is a great region for hunting we saw absolutely no game. The animals were far too wary to show themselves. All the

wildlife encountered here was clump after clump of pride-of-the-mountain, a pentstemon with sprays of large pinky-mauve flowers like Canterbury bells, growing on rocky ledges, and though these excited me they left Lee quite cool and calm.

At Elko on the Elk River, a flat tire permitted us to visit the canyon and the falls while it was repaired. Elko, though it looked like a movie wild west town with the population in character parts, was absolutely authentic. Our mechanic asked, "You folks from New York? Some sportsmen here after grizzlies, they come from a famous island out there."

"Long Island?" Lee said.

"No, not that one. You know—Coney Island!"

I rather resented those Coney Island sportsmen and felt I'd rather have the grizzlies chase them, in a nice way of course, than the other way round.

West of Elko the logged-over hills were tattered and bleak. Then we entered the Yahk Forest Reserve (which had pine hills, parklike, with grassy glades), met the Kootenay River, came down into a wide valley, and spent the night at the town of Cranbrook.

The following day was filled with a steady, unremitting rain. The air was damp and warm, like spring air in the south, for this was the interior Wet Belt of western Canada, where the precipitation varies from thirty to sixty inches a year. (The Coastal Wet Belt is even more humid, with a rainfall which may reach one hundred and twenty inches.) We planned a side trip to see Kootenay Lake, coming back to Cranbrook that night. Though we took the trip we saw very little of Kootenay Lake; the rain and fog defeated us.

But for some reason, or no reason, I didn't care at all. I was in the strangest dreamy state that day. Perhaps it was the warm humid air after the sparkling atmosphere at Waterton; or perhaps the ceaseless rainfall, straight and steady, had a hypnotizing effect.

I had a feeling that I was in an unknown dimension of time and space. Nothing was related; I was both literally and figuratively in a fog. The light was always dark, if I may put it that way, so that we had no impression of morning, noon, or evening. The rain fell in long beaded curtains, perfectly straight; there was no wind, yet black clouds went tearing furiously across the gray mist above us.

There were no mountains to be seen, though this was a mountain road. Steep forest rose to disappear in vagueness. And the trees were foreign to me. Larches, not at all like the tamaracks of the swamps, were lofty giants here, and their newly budded twigs seemed wrapped in green chenille. From their wide fronds the cedars might have been related to tropical tree ferns.

Since then I have read in *Forestry in Canada* that "the principal species in this region are Englemann spruce, western red cedar, western hemlock and Douglas fir. Among other species . . . are alpine and grand firs, western white pine and western larch. Lodgepole pines commonly replace stands destroyed by fire. Black cottonwood is found on rich alluvial soils." But at the time I felt not the slightest trace of my usual curiosity to identify any of them.

In an amiable daze I enjoyed the luxuriant growth, especially the small spruce with new shoots upturned like Christmas candles and ornaments of shiny little cones. I hardly knew whether we were in a car or a motorboat, there was such a wake behind us. Our road was as wet as the flooded river alongside, though not as turbulent. Yet when we left the car to peer at a lake, half-hidden by clouds which swung low across it, the sides of the car were almost dry, so rapid is the rate of evaporation in this region.

It was almost like reaching a harbor when we came into Creston, which, garlanded in blossoms, looked as if it were a Riviera town. Apple trees, rosy May trees, lilacs, honeysuckle, and roses spread their fragrance through the fog, and daisies and dandelions gave a little sunlight to the dark day.

But in the valley the Kootenay River was in flood, and at the lake the fog became so dense we could not see across the valley. The road was being repaired and had turned into a quagmire; the lake was a gray nothing before us. We turned around.

Our way back to Cranbrook was rainier than ever. The spruce were black blobs against sullen gray, and raindrops pounded angry little fists on our car roof. There was no scenery. Just straight trunks going up and rain coming down.

Splashing along the dark road made us sleepy, and we decided to explore on foot. Wandering into the forest, away from the flooded river, to our surprise we found the porous soil was scarcely wet. On pine needles and resilient moss it was delightful walking, and the damp air was balmy and refreshing.

Under tremendous larches, sometimes thin and spare like futuristic trees, and sometimes with feathery plumes of foliage, or under firs whose coquettish little fans were newly tipped with bright emeralds, I felt as we went through the mist as if we were walking on the bottom of the sea. It really was a stony sea, of course, for the roughly parallel mountain ranges, running from the southeast to the northwest, are actually rising and falling, as the great tides rise and fall, though in motion infinitely slow.

But that was not what I felt. I felt mermaidish, enveloped in a pleasant watery world; the light seemed an undersea greenish one, and the clouds that sealed us in were above us like waves on the surface of the ocean.

Under aqueous branches we came to a grassy pond. But there was so little difference in the density of its water and what was falling around us that I couldn't help feeling that the duck families swimming on the lake and the flocks of mountain bluebirds in the air were really schools of strange fish, and some Canada geese asleep in the rain with their heads tucked under their wings looked as closed up as so many feathered oysters.

Most of the ducks here were mergansers. A hen came steaming along with a brood of ducklings, one fortunate baby on her back looking most superior. There was also a large party of older ducklings, about thirty of them, with no mother to guide them. And how they were enjoying it, as they ran along the pond to slide into the water with tremendous splashes.

114

One merganser kept her dozen in a tight formation, two or three standing on her back, the others wedged as tightly behind her as if they rode on a long tail. The family certainly was a unit. I think the mother was a young thing and this was her first responsibility. A matron with twenty was more debonair. Perhaps the reason for her carefree attitude was that the chicks did not all belong to her, for sometimes several broods combine to form one large family. At any rate, the children were allowed to scatter far and wide, raising little fountains all over the pond as they made energetic dives after food.

Lee decided he would try to make his way around the pond and see if he could get closer to the geese. I sat down under the loftiest of the spruces, curled in my waterproof cape, snug and dry; the green-starred moss made thick cushions around me and I leaned back against the rough trunk and looked far up through repeated patterns of spiky needles. I liked this—I had often walked in the rain, but I couldn't remember that ever before had I sat relaxed and at peace in the midst of a rainstorm.

There has been so much written of the comfort one feels in lying on the ground, close to Mother Earth, and far too little of the satisfaction it is to lean against the trunk of a great tree. Here is the same feeling of *belonging*, with an added sensation of protection—yes, and something else. I always feel that a huge tree is both touched and amused when we lean against it, as we would feel if a tired chipmunk rested its head against our foot. Deeper than that, real companionship flows between us; there is an ancient and enduring bond between man and tree.

The rain was still pouring down with mistaken persistence the next morning. We started north from Cranbrook along the Rocky Mountain Trench; this valley, from two to fifteen miles wide, runs for nine hundred miles between the great ranges of the Selkirks and the Rockies. Over a hundred miles north, at Radium Springs, the Windermere-Banff Highway would lead us east over the Rockies again, to Lake Louise and Banff. I had secret qualms about taking that mountain road, for surely, if it had rained so violently in this valley, the passes must be drifted with heavy snowfalls.

As the morning mists began to vanish and Cranbrook was behind us, we seemed to be driving into some giant's hall. Its blue-black walls were mottled with snow, mats of white clouds spread out from its canyons, and its ceiling was a flat gray fog. As Lee remarked disparagingly, the ceiling was also a leaky one.

However, the ceiling gradually lifted, broke apart, and blew up over the mountain walls in rags and tatters. Once more we had white summits towering from the southern horizon to the northern one, only now they were not to the west of us as they had been at Waterton, but on the east. Our road ran through open country dotted with black stumps. Through thin remnants of pines the wind moaned faintly.

After driving fifty miles and passing the village of Skookumchuck (that would be a difficult address to give nonchalantly) we went along the Kootenay River, which was almost up to the road. By Canal Flat it was well out of its banks and a queer, cloudy, dangerous color; men were watching at the bridge.

Just a little way on, a tiny stream ran into Columbia Lake. It was the source of the great Columbia River, and Lee said that if he had a shovel he would be tempted to dig a ditch between this thread of brook and the Kootenay, and disrupt the whole northwest.

The Columbia and the Kootenay part in the marshy meadow, where they are only these few rods apart. As the Kootenay makes a detour into the States (where it is spelled Kootenai), the Columbia takes a long journey into the north and returns south through large lakes. There, after the Kootenay joins it as a tributary, it enters the United States as one of our great rivers, and through a gorge in the Cascade Range it comes down to the sea.

As a brook, the Columbia went through a grassy marsh to enter the lake of pale turquoise, and Canada geese were all through the shallows; it was odd to hear their honking mixed with the notes of song spar-

rows. Along the west side of the lake was sand-hill country, with high dunes, pines, and sparse desert grasses. Recrossing the Columbia beyond the lake—where it was a creek hidden in underbrush—we passed by Fairmont Springs and came to Radium Hot Springs and the entrance to Kootenay Park and the Rockies.

Once more the clouds lifted and we could see that the forests above us on the mountain side were heavy with snow. I was more reluctant than ever to start up to the pass; if we didn't skid we would surely stick in drifts. But at the information booth they told us that this road was preferable to the Crowsnest, where we had crossed the Rockies two days before. There the Fernie Bridge was expected to go out at any moment.

We went through the gates and up a narrow canyon. The color was startling. Brilliant orange crags overhung the green torrent of Sinclair Creek, and even just above us the pines were a frosty glitter. The slopes were deep in new snow.

But our road remained clear, and after we got over the first pass, which was less than five thousand feet in elevation, there were fewer fresh drifts. The road led into a mountain valley bright with orange-green muskeg. Snow made the ridges on either side of it immaculately white and beyond stretched vistas of purple-black ranges with silver crests. Storm clouds added an ominous note. For forty miles the Kootenay ran through this lonely valley.

On a bare hillside, above burned forest, Lee stopped to get sketches of dead pines. The storm-threatened region looked like good moose country, and I began to scan it with my field glasses. No moose on that ridge, nothing at all in the valley. A huge bare shoulder of a mountain blocked the northeast and I swept casually over it. Then I stopped being casual.

Five white spots were on a dome jutting out from that shoulder. Those spots were goats. Mountain goats. They must be, from their environment. And I had found them all by myself.

I shrieked at Lee and he came running, expecting to see me in hand-to-hand combat with a wolf pack, at the very least. More and more of the spots were scattered all over the perpendicular faces of the rock, until the count came to more than forty, grazing on slanted trails or sticking incredibly to the wall as if they were bewhiskered barnacles.

Forty mountain goats at our first sight of them! This was a truly remarkable number to find together; they are supposed to go in bands of from a half-dozen to a score or so.

We were a long way from the animals, but our road led into a valley that skirted the shoulder, and we found ourselves closer to them, though far lower. We could see the heavy bodies hunched at the shoulders, the absurd ankle-length pants, and the long solemn faces as they tilted their heads to look down on us.

They walked with great deliberation—goats do not bound as the sheep do, they amble. But this gait, though it looks mechanical rather than graceful, gets them wherever they want to go. Their black hoofs have chisel edges which can cut into ice if they do not get too worn, and the center is a rubber cushion such as the mountain sheep have, which has the ability to fit tightly into crevices and stick.

When these goats climb they do not leap as the sheep do, but lift themselves up. W. T. Hornaday in his delightful *Campfires in the Canadian Rockies* has an account of four goats climbing a wall, the angle of which seemed only a few degrees from the perpendicular, while the footholds were mere edges and small knobs no bigger than a fist. Yet each goat went practically straight up. "The powerful front legs performed three-fourths of the work . . . reaching up until a good foothold was secured, then lifting the heavy body by main strength. . . . Often a goat would reach toward one side for a new foothold, find none, then rear up and pivot on its hind feet, with its neck and stomach pressed against the wall, over to the other side."

I saw one old fellow fast asleep on such a narrow ledge that I could only hope he would not start up suddenly from a nightmare. There seemed no way for him to have reached that ledge, or to escape from it, except by flying. It began to rain where we stood, but the clouds tearing past that stony rampart were speckling it with snow. The goats did not mind. For their coats, which consist of woolly underfur and a long hairy overcoat, are shaggy and thick enough to be impervious to snow or sleet; it is heat rather than cold which makes them uncomfortable.

Impossible as it sounds, these goats are really mountain antelope. In the geographical scale, they rank highest among the mammals. They

121

choose to live above timberline, where they eat moss and lichens if grass and brush are not available, and look out upon the world in lofty silence. Their dispositions seem to be calm and sober; they keep their heads when hunted (at least they try to) and often escape by remaining motionless instead of taking to panic flight.

But their sedate appearance must surely be a solemn mockery, for they are reported to perform the oddest antics. At times they sit up on their haunches with their forefeet dangling, like a bear, and to make themselves look terrible they raise their hair on end as a porcupine does. One writer complains that they walk along the edges of precipices deliberately, even when there is a flat plateau behind them, or will make their way purposefully along a ledge which gives out entirely for a breathless interval of ten feet or so, during which the goats have the appearance of walking on air. They seem to love to peep around corners, and though their long serious faces deny any mischievous intent, I am sure they must have an unholy, carefully hidden sense of humor.

Hornaday believes that "as might be expected of an animal that is born and reared amid appalling danger of many kinds the mountain goat is a creature of philosophic mind. Through sober necessity he is much given to original thinking." He also says that, in fighting, a goat snorts, stamps, and bucks like a bronco. Then, lowering his head till his shaggy beard sweeps the ground, he plunges, and at the psychological moment gives a vicious sideswipe upward with his short horns, to rip open the vitals of his enemy.

"If we're going to Banff tonight, you'll have to give up your goats," Lee said; and we drove on. But we stopped again at Marble Canyon, which, as the guidebook says in an inexplicable burst of understatement, is a gorge of great scenic interest. It is indeed. It is a chasm as the Red Rock Canyon is, but it looks even more as if the earth had suddenly cracked open; for its sides, instead of being scallops of ruby red, are jagged walls of grayish marble, sometimes only two feet or

so apart. Two hundred feet down, a torrent rushes furiously along past deep potholes hollowed out by grinding boulders.

I had been thinking that at last the saskatoon had been outdistanced. But it was only that we were back in earliest spring again. Now in this place I was glad to find it still in the stage of the gray leaf, before the snowy flower.

Spring is the season which brings me the purest ecstasy, but its beauty passes by so quickly that I am always on edge for fear I will miss one or another of its cadences. This spring, however, every melody recurred again and again. The first faint anticipations of green in bud and blade, the delicate emerald mists, then the bright glitter as tiny leaves shook out from pleated folds— these were repeated to us over and over. It is only the greatest art that can bear such reiteration.

And spring was so young, in this young country. The just-awakened feeling was like that of the thirteenth-century lyrics.

> Woods are in leaf again,
>   There is no living thing
> That is not gay again.

This is the spirit of the Canadian spring.

On toward Vermilion Pass we came, not to the deep snowdrifts I had dreaded, but to rivers in flood. I never expected to worry about *floods* on mountain passes! However, after a mild sign warned us to go slowly, we had to ford a stream which came pouring down from the cliffs to cover our road completely.

The highway followed the Kootenay, which, wild and pale, boiled higher and higher, rushing all through the forest in a distracted manner. There was not only water, but a swift current of it, over our road. Our car crept along through it. I felt precariously situated until we came to a parked truck with a bright little campfire somehow built in the middle of the flooded area, where several men, all ready for a rescue in case we were stranded, were having coffee. That was a cheerful sight.

124

We came out of the flood. We reached Vermilion Pass and were in Alberta once more, and (I know this sounds contrived, but it is really true) the sun came out. The spruce forest changed to pine and we saw, glowing in the sunset light, the great castle of stone to the east of us, which showed that we were approaching Banff.

I remembered so vividly the impression Castle Mountain had made on me when I passed through by train that I was thunderstruck to find it had been renamed Mt. Eisenhower. Certainly it is gratifying to have a splendid Canadian mountain named for our great general, but I wish it could have been another peak. This stupendous mass of stone, with its battlements and turrets, its long window slits and arches, can never be anything to me but Castle Mountain.

10.

Banff and the Starry-eyed Blonde

WE ASKED for Carl Rungius' house as soon as we reached Banff. "Go across the bridge," they said, "and turn right along the river. His house is the one with the big studio window."

Banff, situated in the Bow River Valley, circled by spectacular peaks, is of course the best-known town in the Canadian Rockies; it is also one of the most extraordinary. The Canadian government keeps it a trim village, though Banff itself would like to be a big place (which would certainly destroy its special charm). Deer are likely to cross its streets ahead of you, elk chew its aspen trunks, and bear swim its river. At the end of every street looms a giant mountain—the bulk of Stony Squaw, or jagged Mt. Rundle, or Tunnel Mountain. The main avenue ends in the government building, which is like an English manor house with its gardens and spacious grounds; and the Banff Springs Hotel, though huge and ornate, is down around a corner and does not over-shadow Banff itself.

One of the most interesting things about Banff is that Carl Rungius lives there for half the year. As I have said, he is our most famous painter of American big game, and he has studied the animals in the wilderness for many years.

126

Born near Berlin in 1869, he came to America, after studying in German art schools, when he was twenty-five. Depicting animals had always been his great interest, and he began at once to work as an illustrator for sportsman magazines. Soon, however, he was devoting all his time to painting. At first he had a studio at Greenpoint, Long Island, and spent summer and fall in the field in New Brunswick. But Jim Simpson, a famous Canadian guide, happened to see a Rungius painting of Dall sheep and was so enthusiastic about it that he invited the artist to Alberta to study .the Big Horn.

Rungius fell in love with the Canadian Rockies, and since then has spent half of each year in Banff and the wild country surrounding it.

He is a field artist—"I have to go out in the wilderness," he says. "Zoo animals have not the proper carriage"—and in his pictures he aims to depict the animal and its environment as one whole. For years he made a portrait of every specimen he shot and so got not only the appearance of the species but the particular characteristics of individuals. He has also made studies of hundreds of landscapes.

Though he likes to go out on pack-train trips with companions, for serious hunting and study he goes alone or with his guide. He is a master camper, having fifty years' experience behind him, and takes great pride in being able to be as comfortable on a mountain peak or in a desert canyon as at home.

After crossing the Banff Bridge, we followed a river path through pine trees, glancing at each house across the road. Around a slight curve, we saw a moose standing in the path just ahead of us.

"Carl's house must be there; that moose is certainly an appropriate signpost," Lee said. "Yes, there's the fence he had to build to keep the elk out of his garden."

Carl Rungius met us with as much cordiality as if we had been life-long friends, and it was delightful to sit and talk about big game in his studio while we looked at the many horns and skulls which ornamented the big room and its balcony, or gazed out at the lodgepole pines and the mountains framed by the high studio window.

He showed us a striking painting he was at work on—a herd of elk on an autumn hillside—exhibited with pride his cases of collected butterflies, and took us out to see his Alpine garden, with wild forget-me-nots, alpine primroses, and many other plants which he had brought back from the heights.

Small, wiry, and strong as a hickory knot, he still has a spring in his step and a glint of boy-mischief in his eye. Though he is more than seventy-five, he talked with infinite zest about his recent hunting and camping trips and of swimming horses through the icy rivers. "I'd be an old man if it wasn't for those trips," he said vigorously.

Though he has spoken English fluently for many years, he still clings to some individual expressions. "What do you most enjoy painting?" someone once asked him. "Mooses in spruces," he said with a gleam in his eye.

One evening we were watching a sunset sky, curling and shifting from molten gold to rose and copper over high snows that were shadowed to a violet-gray. "The cold snow and the warm sky," was all Rungius said, but we could hear the emotion he felt, in spite of his noncommittal tone.

We felt fortunate in being introduced to the Banff country by its great portrayer. This year the snowfall had been exceptionally heavy, and all around the springtime green in the valley the icy ramparts pitched and soared into the heights of heaven. We went up the Sundance Canyon to watch for elk and beaver, saw the Banff Springs Hotel full of Pacific Coast lumbermen at play, and met deer in the woods and hoodoos near Tunnel Mountain.

Though the mountains of this park are impressive enough in mid-summer, they are far more glorious and violent when they are sheathed with snow, as we were seeing them. Many of the peaks, like titanic edifices—palaces, fortresses, and cathedrals—are composed of millions of tons of rock material once deposited in layered beds and now towering thousands of feet in weird façades or sharply tilted peaks. To the east of the town the Bow River cuts a great gorge between ranges, out into the plains.

After spending a few days in Banff, we found a mountain cabin halfway between Banff and Lake Louise, at Johnson Canyon. Standing among lodgepole pines, whose straight trunks swayed gently in the windy air, it was small, snug, and immaculate, with a wood stove and snowy cotton blankets instead of sheets to keep us warm. A note pinned to the wall mentioned that it was unwise to put eatables on our porch or in the windows, as a bear might tear the screen and go off with the provisions. He might also come in after them, I supposed.

We could see both Castle Mountain and Pilot Mountain from our door. Castle Mountain was most breath-taking in the sunrise light, its massive walls of a warm pinkish-yellow, its long gothic windows and great parapets topped with snow that was transformed into a rosy radiance. Pilot Mountain, a grand bulk to the south, a good old primitive fortress that stood as a landmark to early explorers, was equally glorious at sunset.

We settled down here for a while, to take the spectacular scenery for granted as a background to daily living, to run over to Lake Louise for dinner, drop into Banff to see Carl, or drive over the Great Divide to the unique Spiral Tunnels.

This last trip was a favorite one, for it combined wild scenery, wild flowers, and wild railroading. The highway led up through pines on the Alberta side, into the spired spruces of British Columbia, till we met the Canadian Pacific tracks along the Kicking Horse River.

The highway here ran on the old railroad right of way, whose four-and-a-half percent grade had been found too steep for practical operation. The present track has a two-and-two-tenths percent grade; this was made possible by building a much longer track and by recklessly blasting into the mountain slopes to make two spiral tunnels, each one of which is three-fifths of a mile long. I did not mind how long we stopped on our road high above this track, to watch the trains climb up from Field and curve, in what is almost an elongated figure 8, in and out of mountains.

Mt. Stephen, which loomed commandingly above the canyon, had a special fascination for me among all the peaks in the Banff region, and we longed to explore Yoho valley, to the west, but its roads were still blocked. Sometimes we drove on down to Field and had lunch in that little station's pleasant dining room, which always had fresh linen and bouquets of wildflowers on its tables, while we watched the freight trains start up the long climb, their heavy exhausts reverberating in the air, or marveled at occupants of passenger coaches who were reading funnies with no regard for the magnificence all about them.

I gloried in the wild color of the Kicking Horse River, running apple-green with pinkish shallows, its emerald banks studded with preposterously huge and yellow dandelions. Between purple-blue hills it ran far down the valley until it joined the great Columbia.

Snowdrifts kept us from revisiting our Moraine Lake, but Lake Louise was as strangely exquisite as ever. It is a real achievement for her to remain as alluring to us as the more remote lakes! Though now, of course, the great hotel was empty, as if it were an ancient cliff dwelling, and we had the paths around the lake all to ourselves.

We walked at sunset along the shores among tall spruces and looked up through their boughs into forests as wild as if no well-trodden trails were below it. Lake Louise seems made of a strange liquid substance, not opaque yet not transparent; a shifting mixture of jewel color— turquoise, sapphire, emerald, amethyst, jade—translucent, tantalizing, never the same two minutes together.

It lies in an amphitheatre hollowed out by glacial pressure. To the south is Victoria Glacier with Mt. Victoria crystal-white in the background. It was covered by a huge weight of snow in the Ice Age and

132

glaciers descended from it, gouging out the great cup for Lake Louise. The hotel stands on the frontal moraine, made of boulders and sand brought down by the glacial ice, and this barrier holds the lake in place, five hundred feet above Banff.

We went along the shore to the glacier's gap, revelling in the smell of the deep forest. We met porcupines at intervals, decidedly put out at our advent and seeming to think the world had taken a turn for the worse. But the song of the russet-backed thrush made us welcome, and as we climbed up over the steeper portion of the trail, the lovely white dryas blossoms made us feel we were renewing a friendship, for we had found them before when we visited Lake Louise.

Scrambling up a huge rock slide, I said, "This is just the kind of a place we found at Moraine Lake. Where the hoary marmot was, and the rock bunny."

We had once spent a week in the Valley of the Ten Peaks, and all the time we were there Lee became violent whenever I called this pika a bunny. He never seemed to realize I did it on purpose to hear his horrified tone. Now, ten years later, "Don't call the rock rabbit *that*," he protested with indignation. "It's a fine little animal."

As he spoke there was a high squeaky bark, almost like "Pee-Ka," which is the unmistakable note of the rock bunny; and on a wedge of rock before us sat the odd little creature, like a baby rabbit with round mouselike ears.

The pika (Little Chief Hare, the Indians call him) does not belong to the rabbit family; he has one all his own. He is supposed to be very shy, but this one did not seem timid. He sat like a gray lichen on his stony perch till we were quite close and then ran off, taking short hops across the broken rock. The dense fur on the soles of his feet made him as sure-footed as the mountain sheep.

These rock rabbits are found at or above timberline. They are day-light animals, though their peculiar barks are sometimes heard at night. In late summer they are busy little haymakers, cutting down grass and

133

flowers which they carry in large bundles and spread on the rocks to dry. The little haystacks they store under ledges for use in the wintertime, as the pikas do not hibernate but remain active beneath the snow in tunnels among the rocks.

"And you said this was a place for hoary marmots," Lee said quite respectfully. "There's one up that slope, almost ready to roll down on you." He was a big gray patriarch, who sat up and gave the clear whistle which is such a part of timberline country.

We watched the afterglow on the mountains and its more brilliant reflection on the lake, and then drove back to our cabin through the black night—a Disney blackness, with round eyes in it.

Now we were at the height of spring. The beauty was excessive, the intensity hardly bearable at times. The surge of leaf and flower was a tide so high that I was almost swept off my feet by it. How could anyone think that herbage was static! Especially since I had read Platt's *This Green World*, I was far more sensitive to the headlong propulsion in each plant, as it lifted great weights of water, created food, set buds for next year while this year's were just expanding. Even in the flower itself the activity was vehement as the petals unfolded and faded, pistils and stamens rose and fell according to the needs for reproduction, and millions of most intricately patterned pollen particles were made and scattered to the winds.

The flowery climax for me was on one pearl-gray evening when I wandered into the forest by myself. A twilight wind was deliciously fresh and delicate and just touched with the faintest pine fragrance. I went down a hillside where gnarled pines were standing knee-deep in the creamy swirls of last year's grass, and came to a swamp, with deep muskeg and distorted stumps scattered black and goblinlike. Here among the pine needles and bearberry vines, I found the delicate rose-and-purple-and-gold flowers of the little calypso orchids.

I had seen several once in the Adirondacks and had felt most triumphant, since they are said to be one of the rarest and most beautiful of our native orchids. Now I encountered, not one or two, not several, but uncounted hundreds of the lovely little flowers, like small lady's slippers, standing in the clear green twilight. In their small perfection, the exquisite color contrast, the restraint they showed in having only one round green leaf—somehow they seemed the most individualistic of flowers. Each seemed to keep its own fascination, its own personality, even when they were gathered close together in great colonies.

In this early June, meadows and forests were alive not only with greenery. The winds ruffling through the branches rocked myriads of eggs in tiny nests. New birds as well as buds were hatching out on practically every tree. If I stepped over a log a sparrow flew up in my face, and there in a tuft of grass four nestlings were wedged into a woven basket much too small for them. If I sat by the river, a junco almost shoved me aside to feed a disconsolate worm to the two dots of black down waiting between the roots of a stump. In fact, feathered parents were rushing about so breathlessly all day long that they made me feel exhausted.

And there were too many wild animals to be known. Every morning I started out with fresh zest, but I was unaccustomed to being alerted every waking moment, and by evening I began to wish for an hour or two alone. But if, at twilight, we strolled out to look at the railroad track, just as a change from so much wildlife, elk stood like mileposts along it, or coyotes ran across the ties over the trestle. If I took a deer trail, through bushes of the fool's huckleberry (which were covered with little bells, entrancing little urns of creamy pink with scarlet buds) I chased out a bear with her cubs, mother in beautiful black furs and the twins in fuzzy playsuits. If I simply lay back in our steamer chair for a nap under the pines, a small chipmunk with a nut in his paws silhouetted himself, with huge importance, against Castle Mountain and made me laugh.

I also complained about mountains. "Don't you feel worn down at times?" I said to Lee. "They go on being so everlastingly breathtaking. They awe me, they exhilarate me—I understand how John Muir went around shouting aloud on his solitary trips among them. But they never give me a chance to relax—I'm always stretched on tiptoe with exaltation!"

"Well, we'll get you down for a while," Lee said, "We'll drive out on the plains to Calgary tomorrow."

The drive to Calgary was eighty-five miles, and as most of the road was having a major operation it was in a frightful state. I gave a sigh of relief when we finally reached town. We had lunch there and visited the Hudson's Bay Company, which disappointed me a little by being a fine modern department store.

Even from Calgary's outskirts, as we started back across the prairie, we could see the long ranges, and when we reached the open plains fantastic knobs and pinnacles stretched across the horizon from the southeast to the northwest—one hundred and fifty miles of mountains in one glance. In the foreground children were going home from country school on horseback, two or three to every horse.

As we approached the gateway to the park, the makeshift road grew more and more unbearable. My teeth jolted loose, my spine was in fragments. A cold raw wind came, not from the mountains but from the prairie, which seemed an unnecessary insult. I looked at the white peaks which were beginning to shut us in again as icily as they looked at us. I was absolutely through with scenery, I said to myself. It was simply impossible to look at anything more; my mind had acute indigestion from so much high thinking.

Other nature-lovers do not seem to have these sudden revolts—or perhaps they are ashamed to admit it? But after a too prolonged bout of outdoor ecstasy I have been only too grateful to get into the dullest hotel room, pull down the shades so that I do not even have to see the sky, and bury myself in murder mysteries.

Now, to my dismay, the sky was turning to a windy gold. I did not want to have to appreciate one more mountain sunset. Just then Lee said as eagerly as if we had been citybound for weeks, "Let's get out the emergency provisions. We can picnic while we watch the sunset." How could the man! Had he never heard of moderation?

We stopped. Mountain heads stuck up over sharp barricades to peer at us. I felt like a vagrant beetle surrounded by the Ku Klux Klan. They made me nervous; I wanted them to keep their distance. There was too much landscape on each one of them, and every drift of cloud, every flicker of changing light, made a wholly new set of scenery. I was not strong enough to cope with it all.

I said without the least interest, "Do the mountain sheep make all the little paths that terrace these hills?"

"Heavens, no, not down at this level," Lee said.

Just then around a curve between the pine trees above us, came five handsome mountain sheep with great curls of horns. They turned to look at us placidly and then began to feed. Hurriedly we snatched our field glasses.

The rams looked as if they had just been sculptured, as the last rays of the sun brought out their clotted coats in heavy relief. We could see every detail of their stocky forms, strong legs, and tiny hoofs. The largest ram had horns of a deep ivory color that made a full arc, springing up from the top of the head to make a bold curve backward, then outward and forward, and curled up at the tip again. It was a great joy to study these magnificent heads, the structure of the curving

horns and the way they were set upon the head, the beautiful yellow eyes.

The five moved in unison, always facing the same way. Sometimes they were abreast, close together; sometimes as they moved uphill they spread out to graze. Never in the world had I expected to see mountain sheep in such detail and at such length. We did not move until they disappeared over the brow of the hill, the big ram in front, the others two by two in military precision.

But this was not all our good fortune. As we drove on, we came upon two more rams on a ledge, just by our road, only eight or nine steps from us. We stopped the car and there we were face to face. Their glorious golden eyes looked into ours with benign serenity.

No wonder big-game hunters feel that these animals excel in romantic glamor. Mounted specimens give no idea of their beauty. All their character lies in their vitality, the life power ennobles them to an infinite extent.

As Lee tried to catch their postures on paper, they walked leisurely around a jutting rock, leaped as lightly as deer up a perpendicular crag between low pines, and came out on the top, where they looked down at us.

I wished, thinking of the stories of their power to descend vertical walls, that something would make them leap down the precipice. For their skill in making use of the smallest irregularities, when they are bounding down dizzy chasms which it seems impossible for them to descend, is so incredible that it results in folk tales of the animals leaping off into space and alighting on their curved horns. After which feat, I suppose, they might rock back and forth on them.

Though such stories are untrue, it is a fact that in fighting, two rams will challenge each other and then run head on, crashing together in a manner calculated to induce severe concussion. I must say that is a duel I would like to see.

But if I had to choose between that excitement and the experience we had of looking deep into the clear golden eyes of those mountain rams, I would choose the latter. There I found the spirit of the high mountains, and in the power and gallant serenity of those eyes I forgot all about my small exhaustions and met dignity with dignity.

Our last day in the Banff region started out as a depressing one. When we woke, rain was tapping noisily on our roof and the pine branches drooped and dripped disconsolately.

But since it was our last day, we decided to find a moose lick which Carl Rungius had described to us. He had told us in the height of his evening enthusiasm that moose often congregated at this place, and I understood him to say there were so many that he had to lean against one in order to sketch another. Even though he denied this statement in the cold light of next day, I wanted to see the spot.

The mountain road which had been so brown and wintry when we first drove over it was now a rainy green, and after Vermilion Pass the air was warmer, with a damp fragrance. Waterfalls trailed like filmy ghosts along every dark escarpment, and up past the misted spruce tops the ranges were a profound and thoughtful blue.

In one opening in the woods we saw an enormous black bear out for a stroll in the rain, and followed his example. But not in the same clearing.

Under the spruce boughs which had been pressed downward by the weight of many winter snows were juniper and laurel. I found white bunchberry flowers, scattered like big squared snowflakes through the moss, the tiny vines of cranberry and minute ivory dots, neatly folded, which absolutely refused to open into my cherished one-flowered pyrolas, no matter how exasperated my gaze became.

Stately pines were weaving very slowly in the wet wind. The silence was profound. A single bell note from an invisible grosbeak finally broke the stillness and we followed it to a hobgoblin thicket, where the dead spruce branches curled like claws and gray moss hanging from them seemed hanks of witches' hair. I was relieved to reach green forest again.

As we approached the moose lick, we were surprised at its size. It was quite a large pool, hollowed out by the moose as they licked the salty mud, and sheltered by close thickets and the forest edge.

In it stood an enormous bull moose. He was a magnificent creature, by far the biggest I had ever seen. When he caught sight of us he moved off behind the spruce in a casual fashion, but as we remained quiet he soon came back to the pool again. These salt licks have an amazing drawing power.

He was a finely formed animal, powerfully muscled and at the height of his strength. His coat was smooth; he had shed his winter hair. His shoulder hump was massive and the pendulous bell under his throat

was like a heavy beard. His horns had grown out appreciably and were horizontal shelves over his small eyes; we could see the velvety plush on them and though they looked swollen and tender to the touch, he scratched a hind leg vigorously with one antler, while he held another leg over his head—the neatest trick of the week.

The moose is the least polygamous of the deer family, though there seems to be grave doubt as to whether he is as monogamous as some early writers believed. In the autumn the bulls roar and the cows, instead of being modest and reticent, call just as urgently. We once heard a cow moose in the night, on a canoe trip in Ontario, and it remains with me as the weirdest sound I ever heard, far more so than the howling of the wolves.

When alarmed, moose can travel at a rapid trot for many miles, and they swim for great distances. Their necks are so short they cannot reach the ground without spreading their forelegs apart as giraffes do, and the great platters of horn with spiny edges, which serve as antlers, rank high on the list of peculiar adornments among the mammals. Long ago both Pliny and Caesar reported on the moose with some odd fancies about him. He was supposed to walk backwards when grazing because his upper lip was so long. And because he had no joints in his legs, he never lay down, poor lamb, but reclined against a tree whenever he slept. I would like to come upon such a sleeping beauty.

Our big bull was wide awake, and we had no sooner congratulated ourselves on seeing him than we caught sight of movement in a marsh beyond us. Soon a cow and calf came out, both with such long legs that they surely must have had a touch of giraffe in their blood. The young moose, though last year's calf, was still babyish, innocent and gawky, with a tiny stiff ruff and a mite of a dewlap.

The two waded out into the water to drink, and several elk who had been mere shadows in the forest stepped forth timidly. Then as a truck splashed by on the rainy road they vanished; mom and baby took to the woods likewise, the youngster stumbling in his flurry.

But as the bull did not move, the others came back; and then to our satisfaction, two more moose appeared. They were adult, but they certainly had far to go before they reached the dignity of our big bull. They were thin and bony, with very hooked noses; instead of a big bell, they had ridiculous black strips of hairless hide that swung limply in the wind. In shedding, mats of hair, several inches deep, had fallen off and left patches of bare skin so they looked piebald as well as unkempt. The horns of one were narrow laths with knobbed ends, the other had two silly little fans on his head. The callow pair walked into the pond and drank noisily.

Then from over the hill, down a trail through the thicket, came hurrying a young moose all in silver gray. I had heard there were no albino moose; I never thought before that a moose could be really beautiful. She was both, with her immaculate coat varying from iron-gray to silvery tones and her soft ruff almost white. She was breathless: she had *just* remembered this cocktail party and *dashed* over. She must have swum a river in her haste, for she shook showers of water-drops from her coat as she made her appearance.

And she really made an appearance. When the other moose drank, they straddled or waded belly-deep into the water. But Silvery, after her rush to join the party, stood still till everyone saw her. Then she dropped on her slender knees to drink fastidiously. A moment later she stood up, then even more delicately went down on one knee at the edge of the pool.

She certainly had style, from her pointed black hoofs to the tips of her spirited ears. Her nose was practically straight, her head moved alertly instead of swinging in a heavy fashion, she actually had a viva-cious look. And how she did pose—Lee called her the starry-eyed blonde.

Even as she drank she looked sideways as if to see if she was attract-ing the attention she deserved. Mom kept her at a distance, the sedate matron had no patience with her tricks and manners. Silvery was a little afraid of Mom.

Five elk, all does, came out of the woods; they were more graceful creatures than Silvery, with their lovely arch of neck and slender aristocratic heads. But it was she who had the allure. She was a femme fatale if ever a cow moose was one.

Another car went by on the road, and Silvery decided to pretend she was afraid. She ran to the side of the big bull, twice her size, for protection. He allowed her to stay until the car disappeared, then swung his great head viciously at her. There was no time for dalliance in his life now.

She scurried off in alarm. She went over to a tangle of drenched bushes and there she sulked. She really did, it was not just an idea of mine. Her ears were laid back and her whole expression was disgruntled.

The party went on without her, however, and soon she was back in the midst of the festivity. The drinking that went on there was scandalous, nothing less. It was unbridled.

I don't believe that forest pool in the mountains will ever cease to be vivid to me. I never had such an atavistic feeling as these animals gave me. I thought at the time it was because moose, of all creatures, seem to belong to the past rather than to the present.

But now I wonder. Perhaps we went back further than I knew, into a mythological past? Was Silvery a moose after all? A unicorn doe may not have a spiked horn on her forehead as the stags do. Perhaps what we saw that rainy day was a young she-unicorn?

11.

By Way of the Ice Age to Jasper

OUR small cabin was dark under pines and stars when we came home that night. I welcomed every little star, for we were driving up to Jasper the next day by way of the Columbia Ice Field Highway.

This highway, which has been open only for a few years, is one of the most glorious in the world. For one hundred and eighty-six miles, between Banff and Jasper, it cuts northward through the wildest and heretofore most inaccessible country: over Bow Pass, down to the Saskatchewan River, up over Sunwapta Pass, down to the Athabaska, and so to Jasper. I could hardly wait till it was time to start and, since we were eager for a perfect June day, we looked at the star-studded sky with complacency.

But alas, the next morning our alarm clock was the trampling of raindrops on the roof, and we drove away in a foggy, foggy dew. At the Lake Louise Forks we turned north and took the highway to Jasper.

The tall Engelmann's spruce were beautiful in the rain. Lakes lay like flat ornaments of turquoise and jade, set in the forest. Our road

went uphill, with little illegitimate waterfalls, nameless and rowdy, falling off the stony knees of disapproving mountains.

In the heavy forest the pyrolas were in bloom at last, in vast quantities, the single-flowered ones complete with their lily-of-the-valley fragrance, the others in pink and ivory sprays.

The ground was covered with green billows—billows of the exquisite fern moss, made up of miniature fronds. This had so delighted me when I first found bits of it in the east; but there I had had to *hunt* for it, I now told myself incredulously, as I gazed on its interminable interlacings covering hollows, logs, and rocks, and thatching little dens under upturned stumps, decorated with twinflower vines and yellow violets. In the green cathedraled spaces, small firs looked quaint and childish. Somewhere on a hidden lake a loon laughed wildly.

The weather became uncertain of its mood. We began to have glimpses of clear peaks and others muffled to the chin in clouds. Stone gargoyles stood on the sheer mist. No-See-Um Creek was full of boulders and sunshine, but Mosquito Creek was swept with rain. At Crowfoot Glacier the woods below us were snowdrifted; there were long paths made by snowslides, with globeflowers blooming in between.

Our road became stranger and stranger. The few white peaks that were visible floated in the mist like bodiless heads. And now of course when it was difficult to see the mountains, instead of feeling relieved, I could not bear to miss a single one. I had found my second wind and was eager for more and more towering ranges.

Bow Lake, which is the headwaters of the river flowing through Banff, was a most vivid turquoise. Three harlequin ducks were diving through this molten mineral, the straight spruce stood in silence about it, and mule deer with their antlers almost grown wandered here and there.

Raindrops accompanied us again. As we went higher, the bushes receded from leaf to bud and finally to only a glint of gold-green tip.

The grass was brown. We reached the summit of Bow Pass at 6,785 feet. This is not high, compared with Colorado mountain passes, for instance, which may be eleven or twelve thousand feet, and we had no feeling of height. Instead, we felt we had suddenly taken a step in seven-league boots to the Arctic Circle.

The summit was an open plateau, almost tundra country, with low willows; and the brown bushes tipped with silver-gray pussy willows made the area look like a grizzly's pelt. Stunted woods withdrew until they dwindled into shaggy moss.

More and more storms streamed down. We were going through the most violent splendor and we could get only snatches of it. Because we had mere glimpses, the grandeur was really terrifying; mostly there was the substance of cloud around us, through which a black unmanageable cliff rose, plunging and rearing from restraining snow, or above the dark squalls a frozen shaft stabbed up into faint light.

A colossal dome might overshadow us, with black forest cowering in the crevices. Desolate walls and pinnacles loomed immensely higher because we could see racks of clouds floating about in the gulfs of space beneath them.

Once when Lee stopped to make a note of a cloud effect, I climbed out over rocks to stand at the edge of a chasm. From there I gazed out across a sea of tumbled storm clouds and fierce peaks, tossing in a haggard half-light. Always before this, whatever vagaries a landscape offered, I had felt sure of the globe's stability beneath it all. But now the bones of the earth itself seemed chaotic.

Just below me new leaves glinted, and suddenly on the green treetop there alighted a bit of live flame. It was a rufous hummingbird, brilliantly scarlet, burnished with gold. A tiny torch is what this bird is, fiery without and within. For he has a red-hot temper; he tops the grizzly in ferocity, if not in size, for I do not know of any grizzly attacking an enemy twice his weight, but this hummingbird has been known to battle blackbirds, thrushes, and chipmunks.

He is a valiant arctic explorer too, this three-and-a-half inch mite, ranging farther north than any other hummingbird, breeding in Alaska and the southern Yukon at high elevations. No wonder he dresses in glowing red! His preference for scarlet seems to run through his life; his favorite drink is the nectar of the crimson-flowered currant, after which he chooses red lilies, red columbine, wild honeysuckle, and Indian paintbrush. As I called Lee to see this daring swashbuckler, he buzzed from his poplar twig and disappeared into the foggy gloom, challenging the Rockies.

There were other bits of color now and then. At the Waterfowl Lakes the apple-green water and yellow-green marsh grass were garish, and through the misty rain the Indian paintbrushes bloomed in such flaming brightness that they were like little bonfires all over the wet slopes.

At Mistaya Canyon we walked half a mile to see its black scalloped rock and ice-green water. Bears had clawed the bark of the trees here and the markings were high above my head. They must all be grizzlies here, I said pessimistically. Usually I like to think of the hidden citizens of the country watching us, but here I was too uncabined, unconfined.

And no sooner had we reached the car than a bear did dash across the road, though he was only a chubby cinnamon. It seemed to me that the population of bears in western Canada equaled the human population. It had become quite natural to wonder, whenever I went walking, how near a bear was likely to be.

At the Saskatchekan River crossing, a trading post and pleasant cabins made us decide to stay overnight. Perhaps the next day would be less dour. By suppertime we were justified; the clouds had lifted to show great bare crags where mountain goats should have been. The boy who brought us firewood told us he sometimes saw elk down the hill behind the cabins, and after supper Lee suggested exploring the trail.

Over the slanted earth that towered into snow, a stormy scarlet sky blew into rags and tatters. We walked on and on through the tall grass and brush. It was exciting weather. The atmospheric tensions brought about by storms that were plunging through the dusk made me have the exhilarating feeling that anything might happen.

But as one storm cloud came lowering heavily down our river valley directly toward us, "I think we'd better go back," I insisted, in spite of Lee's urging that we find the end of the path.

It is a good thing that we did turn around, for the trail followed the Saskatchewan and its end was a hundred and fifteen miles away at Rocky Mountain House. Our meandering footpath was the road the Indians took to the Calgary stampedes.

I lay awake that night, thinking of the *depths* of the darkness that lay around us. Mountain valley after mountain valley—what gigantic chalices full to the brim with unbroken blackness! This night was a dense weighted substance, marred by no small man-made glitters or noises anywhere. Except for our few pinpricks of light at this dim river, nothing at all was visible through heavy forest or fearsome labyrinths of stone.

But I was elated rather than cowed by the gloom so solidly massed about our slight shelter. I *liked* the feeling of implacable hostility surrounding us, the frozen cataclysms poised above us, the unseen storms that prowled about the night. I lay and felt the wind shake at our cabin, and thought with deference of the men who had first confronted these savage places and had not turned back.

The new morning was a lofty one. Blue sky was about and up through it the white clouds stood in high towers. We followed the river along burned hills. An elk swam across it to escape from us, but the current brought him down until he landed just alongside.

The day grew clear. Above the gaunt flanks of the hills, fresh snow lay on bastions of ice and slabs of crystal, under a forget-me-not sky. Clouds blew along the lower slopes like smoke from unseen locomotives, and the pale-green river ran through freshly washed forest. "Yesterday was splendid for today," we said joyfully. Even the chip-

munks appreciated the transformation, running along with their tails aloft like triumphal banners.

We passed sandy flats along the river where bleached driftwood lay piled in fantastic carvings for mile after mile. Someone had dropped orange peelings along this solitary road. Orange peelings last. They lie and tell the sordid truth about the humans who leave such litter behind them to spoil the pristine beauty for the next passerby.

Up a mountainside again, the weather had a temperamental fit and attacked us with sleety rain, though the sun still glimmered faintly. Firs stood thickly strung with raindrops; snowdrifts and moss made a mottled carpet broken by ground juniper with its smoke-blue berries and by the pale yellow of the glacier lilies.

We came to the Big Hill and went up the switchbacks to Sunwapta Pass on Mt. Athabaska. This was the steep-pitched section of the road, which people always remember. It was far more exciting than Bow Pass. "Glorious!" said Lee as I tried to look, and tried not to, at the airy depths beneath us.

The road was wide and well-kept, but I wished that it had even the smallest rail or fencing. Just a row of pebbles along the edge would have helped. But the gravel simply stopped and there was emptiness. Far below, the forest offered a halting place.

A far from reassuring sign said: SLIPPERY WHEN WET. "Lucky we didn't come up yesterday," I said happily to Lee. "You don't think it's dry now, do you?" he answered in a preoccupied tone.

Soon there was ice on the wet road, and men working. Working always on the secure inside curve, too, while we, unaccustomed as we were to lofty driving, had to weave around them on the dizzy edge of nothing. We met a grader and I swear the driver, a mere boy to whom I took an instant dislike, deliberately stopped on the narrowest bit of road just to see my expression. I was sorry afterwards I had not hidden it with nonchalant field glasses.

Higher still the road was plowed out through deep drifts, and I relaxed. Snow fenced us in. The clear and flawless fields of white were all about us for miles. Though qualms still squeezed my stomach whenever I looked down, I felt a wild exhilaration sweep through me, as the azure shadows of spruce slanted down the tremendous massive drifts. A hermit thrush sang in the stillness and its poignant notes were as perfect for this high silver as for the shadowy depths of forest twilight.

I had laughed at Lee in Switzerland when he insisted on liking the Rockies better than the Alps because they "hadn't been looked at so much." But now I fully realized what he had meant. The great fascination about these tremendous heights was that they were *unknown*. Only a handful of people, comparatively, have even looked upon them from a distance. No one has ever set foot on many of the peaks. Their imperial highness is not only unconquered, but undefied.

"I think that one of the *properties* of that compound which we call man is that when exposed to the rays of mountain beauty it glows with joy," Muir once wrote. We felt that glow now, more intensely than we had ever known it. Here was white beyond white, new-fallen brilliance and ancient ice-sheathed arcs against gold sunlight. Savage and dazzling slopes swept below us, the stainless turquoise green of the sky was ineffably radiant.

About us was only silence, shining space, and the clean smell of snow. I looked up at drifts overhanging a summit and they were as overpowering in their arrested motion as if a great billow had been frozen just as it was about to break.

At the summit, the boundary between the Banff and Jasper parks, we found a big brown meadow. Clouds closed in on us suddenly and it began to sleet. On a sharp slope a bear came out of a cave in the broken rocks and began to eat grass as if he were one of the ruminants.

To the west were the great peaks that held the Columbia Ice Field. This was the climax of our mountain scenery. I had had no idea that we still had true remnants of the Ice Age left on our continent. Yet here was a cap of ice, one hundred and fifty square miles of it, the last remaining bit of the vast mass which once existed.

When the erosion in the second mountain uplift was still going on, the climate of North America changed. As it became colder and stormier, great quantities of snow fell. The summer sunlight was not strong enough to melt the accumulations of snow and not only were the mountains smothered but great sheets of ice hid much of the plains.

Most of Canada was then covered, and in the Interior Plateau of British Columbia an enormous mass of ice was held between the Rockies and the Coast Ranges. This mass, the weight of which caused immense pressures, moved north toward the Arctic and south into the United States; and the snow was compressed into thousands of alpine glaciers.

From the Columbia Ice Field issue various tongues of ice at the present time. One of the largest is the Athabaska Glacier, and we now came to a side road which led us to its foot. In the foreground a pale stream surged through gravel and rock debris, which had been recently left by the glacier, still moving and constantly receding. For about a mile there was only empty waste. I felt I had slipped back into a prehuman world, and indeed it was a throwback landscape; great portions of our continent once looked like this, as the ice drew back toward the pole leaving only rubble behind it.

But above this desert the glacier soared in white ridges. Caverns of ice, clear and intensely blue, and fringes of long green icicles glittered at its base. Though on each side of us the snow slopes vanished in mist and Mt. Athabaska on our left rose in cloud-veiled grandeur, the Snow Dome and the Ice Field in front of us were sharp-cut against clear sky. It was a strange thing to stand there and realize that the last Ice Age was not quite over, that we are still in the period when ice is shrinking, in a climate such as the waning of other ice ages experienced.

This region is also one of the major drainage divides of North

America, and might be called the apex of the continent. From it the Columbia River flows to the Pacific, the Athabaska River to the Arctic Ocean, and the Saskatchewan to Hudson Bay and so to the Atlantic.

I could not get enough of looking at the silver curve of Dome Mountain. Here, I thought, as we looked past desolate rock to its crystal glory, is absolute remoteness. Here is dark thunder and white silence made manifest.

But at last we turned our backs on the Snow Dome and went along the stream which became the Sunwapta River. The pale milky look of these glacial waters comes, it seems, from rock flour which is ground off by the ice pressure.

Now our car went down sharp hairpin curves and along the river, which dropped seven hundred feet in two miles. Beauty Creek, which was a soft powder-blue, had white heather, singing phoebes, and a bear. Then a long range of mountains tilted to the north and rosy-orange rocks stood in vertical layers. By a small brook, alpine primroses grew in a frail embroidery; and at Sunwapta Falls there were elk about, although they were quite wary.

Again a sudden squall rushed down. Black clouds hid the peaks, the wind roared through the trees. At Athabaska Viewpoint there was a hailstorm. Down below us was a bare cliff terraced by goat hoofs, but we saw no goats though they often visit the place for the salt. To reach this lick they have to walk through thick forest. I wish we could have seen them coming pensively through the trees.

The town of Jasper is situated in grassy parkland, and lakes of varying tints of greenish-blue lie scattered about the valley. David Thompson, an explorer and geographer, crossed the Athabaska Pass in 1811 and opened the Athabaska Trail, which fur traders and adventurers followed for many years. The Hudson's Bay Company and the North West Company fought for control of this trail over a long period; Jasper House was a trading post established in 1813 by the latter company on the Athabaska, which is one of the most important of all Canadian rivers.

When we came into the town, it looked completely deserted. Even the railroad station was locked. But we were not concerned, for we had been asked to stay at a cabin on Lake Edith, with Dr. William Rowan (of the University of Alberta in Edmonton) and his delightful daughter.

Dr. Rowan is a sportsman-scientist, as Rungius is a sportsman-artist. He has been called to teach in many places, but cannot make up his mind to leave his northwest country; it is the prairie stubble shooting, he says, that holds him there. Like Rungius he has a keen sense of humor, though his is sardonic rather than boyish. We had met him briefly at sober scientific meetings in New York, and now his quizzical wit surprised and pleased us, as did the elaborate miniature railroad he operated along the shore of Lake Edith.

Although he is best known for his studies of bird migration, he is a man of many talents: music, painting, sculpture, as well as writing take much of his time. We had a stimulating evening hearing excerpts from a current manuscript on the biology of man; though Dr. Rowan took a dark view of our future, his violent denunciations—of the juke box, for example—were most exhilarating.

The cabin was a picturesque one, on the edge of an aquamarine lake with pines around it. When we walked down to the shore in the late twilight, nesting killdeer flew about us, crying loudly. Two rams walked on the mountain above Maligne River, and we heard geese calling in the night.

The next day, while our host was correcting proof, Lee and I visited Maligne Canyon, which was a deep crack in the mountains as the Marble and Red Rock canyons had been, but this split was pitch black and so far more sinister. The waterfall in this canyon had traveled miles upstream, as it gradually wore away its supporting shelves of rock. The stream had hollowed out deep and threatening caverns in its walls, using boulders as grinding tools. It was a dramatic thing to see, far down between the narrow walls, the river roaring like a captive tempest in black imprisonment.

Under a smaller waterfall, we found the nest of a dipper, or water ouzel, in just the kind of place a dipper is supposed to choose. The little hut of bright green mosses, which looked as if it belonged to a minute Hottentot, was tucked in behind the fall, on a narrow ledge, and silver drops fell before it in a gauzy curtain. The water ouzel herself kept flying down through the black recesses of the canyon and back through the white waterfall to take food to her nestlings.

That noon Dr. Rowan said, "One of the things I've always wanted to find here is a dipper's nest."

"Oh," we said carelessly, "we were looking at one this morning."

Changing the subject rapidly, Dr. Rowan said he could tell us where we might find mountain sheep. We could take a road to Miette Hot Springs.

"Where do we look for them?" I asked.

"You don't have to look," he retorted. "*They'll* look for *you*."

"Really!" I thought.

The Miette road was wonderful. Round bubbles of clouds bounced gaily about the mountains and made garlands on the peaks. At this eastern edge of the park the ranges showed a distortion even more vehement than at Banff. Here the mountains are formed of river-deposited sediments and they almost seem to show a torrent's influence in the static whirlpools and upheavals, in the confusions of petrified surging in the rock strata.

Miette Mountain was a landmark for early explorers and resembles a great fort on a headland. From our road it looked like a tilted fortress as Pisa is a tilted tower.

The road to the springs was splendid, but I became aware that whenever guidebooks call a road magnificent they mean that you look straight down on its scenery. Mule deer along our way looked surprised to see us, with their ears standing straight up like rabbit ears, and on one curve five rams dashed down the road and leaped, as lightly as rabbits, up a steep bank.

Just before we reached the springs we came to a clearing where a score or more of mountain sheep were feeding. It was a pastoral scene. Rams, ewes, and lambs were grazing on tender grass and crisp spring flowers under the scattered pines.

Lee parked the car and got out to take pictures, and I walked down the road toward the trees. On the edge of the highway a ewe and a lamb came to a pile of coal someone had left there, and began to eat it, as greedily as if it were the finest hay. There was a roll of tar paper, too, at which the angular little lamb chewed rapturously. This was no way for wild sheep to behave, and I continued toward the clearing.

A huge ram came toward me. He was coming fast, and in spite of the impression of benignity which he gave, I retreated toward the car.

"*They'll* look for *you!*" Lee shouted, reminding me of Dr. Rowan's words. I kept retreating; I did not want to be butted, however benevolently. But the ram had his head set on coal, not on me. He gleefully joined the munching party.

Others followed him, till soon the whole herd had deserted the daisies and harebells for the sulphur-impregnated coal. Perhaps it was a spring tonic.

I had always had an extravagant admiration for friends who managed to get photographs of mountain sheep; I pictured them risking life and limb, panting up roof-steep peaks, hour after hour, to procure them. Lee's only difficulty, that afternoon, was to photograph the sheep minus the pile of coal and the tar paper.

However, the next morning when we met the Cowans who had a cottage next door to the Rowans—it seems a shame that those names do not rhyme—we found someone who had really seen sheep as they should be seen. Dr. Cowan, of the University of British Columbia, had lived with the Jasper bighorns in their wildest haunts; for five years he had studied them both in summer and winter, and he gave us fascinating bits of information from his intensive knowledge of the animals.

He told us that when the ewes have their young at heel they seek out broken rock cliffs which provide escape terrain, to protect the lambs from coyotes; the rams ignore these predators, so the two sexes range, in summer, over areas of completely different character. The rams, at high elevations, graze on willows which grow knee-high in the mountain valleys and taper off to the minute *Salix nivalis*, all of 1½ inches high, on the upper slopes. This growth, with small sedges and such grasses as sheep fescue and sky-line bluegrass, is the preferred summer food of the bighorn.

"One of the most fascinating days I ever had with the bighorn," Dr. Cowan told us, "was with Jim Simpson, the well-known Rocky

Mountain guide. We climbed a peak which had a series of almost parallel buttresses, each above eight thousand feet in elevation.

"On the highest ridge tops we found a scattering of that mountain rarity, the pigmy poppy, which in itself made the day noteworthy. But of course our main interest was directed toward the sheep; we were making a tally of age groups, sex distribution, number of young, and various details essential to the wild-life biologist, so each flock was carefully stalked, tallied, and left unalarmed.

"I have never, before or since, come upon a summer range so heavily stocked. We tallied 173 rams, 73 ewes and 10 lambs, besides elk, deer, and moose. There were such numbers that our main problem was to approach certain bands while keeping out of the sight and scent of the others, as an alarm would have mixed up the groups and greatly complicated our task. By much crawling and circling we managed to complete our count.

"When we came to the crest of the last ridge we looked over it cautiously and discovered a gaunt old patriarch of a ram sound asleep some thirty feet below us. His massive head was too heavy looking for his emaciated body and his right horn was broken off. I marveled that he could have survived a blow sufficient to break such a horn; as it was, he was battered and worn, and even though it was August, he still carried his winter coat, which is a sure indication of failing vitality.

"He was sleeping soundly as we approached, step by step, until he lay right at our feet. Jim's eyes twinkled, and suddenly he leaped on the ram's back, throwing his arms around its neck. He did not stay on long enough to qualify for a rodeo, but when the ram escaped Jim was left with all its last year's fleece in his embrace, to say nothing of a most sheepish expression."

12.

Hudson Hope Outpost

OUTSIDE the zigzag scarps and buckled upheavals of stone which make the eastern gateway of Jasper a vast fantasy, we headed back at last. Jasper was as far as we were to drive to the west; now we were on the way home. We immediately left the mountains for a wilderness road which led through lonely spruce and muskeg, with poplar-covered hills. We met no cars, only a long-legged coyote face to face and once more the prairie wind.

I remembered that a friend who came from Colorado had spoken of what a pang it always was to leave the mountains behind you. I was loathe to turn my back on their grandeur now, but it was not the wrench to me that it is when I really merge with a region.

Those great presences had kept me astretch with awe and exultation, so that I felt we had been in the presence of the gods. But they were strange gods to me, and I was more at ease seeing the sky on every side of us. Now I had a feeling of release, almost of escape.

From Jasper to Edson, where we stayed overnight, there were marshy solitudes with rarely a house and no side roads at all. Ring-necked ducks and buffleheads were nesting near the scattered lakes, large tamaracks stood in the swamps, and the spruce here had full tops, not tattered ones.

On eastward from Edson the morning air was full of sparkles. Settlements and little farms stood in crystal clarity. Near one of these a highwayman was early abroad. A deer with a bell around its neck stopped us on the deserted road and asked for booty in no uncertain terms.

At Edmonton we had a maddening day, for it was the King's Birthday and everything was closed; we could not even get the mail we had been awaiting ever since we left Waterton. Leaving our car here, we took a train to the northwest, to Dawson Creek.

Dawson Creek sounded like the days of '49 to me; it was the end of the railroad to the Peace River Valley and the actual starting point of the Alaska Highway. An old friend of Lee's from Minnesota had asked us to visit there, and we were delighted at such a chance.

When I looked it up on the map I found that while it is in British Columbia it is farther north than Ketchikan in southern Alaska, farther north than I had ever been. And Lee was pleased to find that our train went by Lesser Slave Lake, even though we passed it in the middle of the night.

As our train averaged the mild speed of twenty miles an hour, the five hundred miles or so took us from 5:30 one evening till 4:30 the next. We were so far north that the night only lasted a couple of hours. At midnight there was still a vivid red sunset glow; the "twilight bow," a luminous curve of light which is a reflection from the sun on high atmosphere, was a new phenomenon to me. There were many stars, a brilliant moon, and, just for good measure, the Northern Lights as well, fringes and swords and spears shaken out in bright array across the sky, undimmed by the strong moonlight.

I could not sleep for this superabundance of glory, and I saw Lesser Slave Lake at 2:30, when a dawn glow was strong in the northeast. Its unbroken pallor lying between hills cut from purple-black struck me as the loneliest water I had ever seen, though I admit I do not often look upon lakes at half-past two in the morning.

Later in the day we were traveling through a most desolate land

162

—burned-over, chopped-over, underbrush country. The towns looked like the more disparaging accounts Dickens gave of early American villages. Along the Smoky River we saw log cabins and barns half-buried in hillsides, some with sod roofs. Fences were sometimes made of dead spruce with their tangled twigs left on them. Pastures were tucked in among burned trees and charred logs. There was rarely even a wagon road to be seen, though in one place we noticed Indians working with graders and four-horse teams.

Over many miles of dismal hummocks our small train grudgingly jolted. Sometimes, for some mysterious reason of its own, it seemed to choose to run on the ties instead of the rails, while passengers were trotted on uneasy seats and baggage popped out of hiding to bark our unsuspecting shins, or tottered drunkenly overhead. The engine had long spells of shuddering, too, and gave unexpected shrieks, no matter how uninhabited the country. As Samuel Johnson once remarked, "All was rudeness, silence and solitude."

But at our speed (though speed is not the word) we were able to observe every detail along the unbalanced track and I could botanize to my heart's content as we bumped around the river's bends. Mile after mile of wild roses, from blush-pink to vivid flame, with off-shades of salmon and cerise, festooned the right of way, and garlands of wild red honeysuckle, purple lupin, and pink laurel-like blossoms hid the banks. Wood lilies, sometimes orange but more often a brilliant scarlet, glittered through the burnings among the black stumps and green grass.

In many places, peat fires were burning in half-cleared tracts. Often a deep layer of black peat lay on subsoil, and as the peat burned down the sand was exposed, with little islands dotted over its level surface, where the moss and peat were too wet to burn. This waste land had an eerie aspect.

The country did not seem as truly wild as British Columbia west of Crowsnest had. Its character, for the most part, was meager, tattered, and forlorn. The hills were knobby; there were few streams and no big trees, only stands of low spruce and aspen.

But after Sexsmith we began to get into the rich Peace River Block and there was a great change. Here were brilliant green wheat fields, pleasant homes, and good dirt roads. This country is very fertile, with record crops of sixty bushels of wheat and one hundred and twenty bushels of oats to an acre. And clearing the land is not difficult or costly, for the growth is sparse.

Grand Prairie had four elevators, a brick school, and houses instead of log cabins. I felt we were in quite a metropolitan area, and our locomotive seemed ill at ease, from its nervous jerks and angry mutterings. As soon as we crossed the boundary from Alberta into British Columbia, there was more water. Streams came down from the hills and marshy ponds with wildfowl were abundant.

At Pouce Coupe, a few miles from Dawson Creek, Ace Comstock and his wife Tiny (so-called because she was more goddesslike than elfin) met us and drove us to Dawson Creek in their car. Although I had never met them before, those few miles began a firm friendship. Ace's enthusiasm for his adopted country was heart-warming, and when I heard how Tiny had run their farm during the war years while Ace was in town, had managed the men, driven tractors, supplied meat (Ace boasted of her skill in getting two bucks one day), and coped with strange emergencies, I added profound respect to my liking.

At first sight, Dawson Creek did look frontierlike. Small houses, many of them very sketchy ones, were strewn around a cup in the bare hills. There were no paved streets, and people clattered along board sidewalks, raised high above the mud, or dust, as the case might be. There were no signs of grass or trees, only a few plants here and there in the bare yards.

Inside the houses, however, there was electricity, running water, and modern heating plants. The Alaska Highway had certainly changed

Dawson Creek, for until the war all the water a householder used was brought to his door in barrels.

As late as the 30's the town consisted only of Wes Harper's store, a co-operative, a blacksmith shop, a garage, and a hotel. When the railroad first came, in 1930, Wes had to jack up his store and move it three miles so that he would not be left out of town. "Women now tell with considerable pride," the Compendium Issue of the *Alaska Highway News* says, "how they came to do their trading. While the egg-crates were being counted and the butter weighed up, and also their lists filled with merchandise, they moved right along with the building. If they stopped long to gossip with Wes, they found themselves a quarter of a mile down the road from their team."

Even after the railroad came, Dawson Creek had only a scattering of houses. But when the Alaska Military Highway was begun, the village mushroomed into a city. It was the railhead; the population increased from eight hundred to ten thousand and the demand for living quarters was so great the golf course was cut up into building lots.

In February 1943, a disastrous fire, caused by a dynamite explosion, destroyed half the town. Wartime secrecy hid the extent of the catastrophe, but temporary structures burned like matches; many people were killed and over a hundred injured. Millions of feet of copper wire stored in the wrecked buildings were blown and tangled about the streets till hose trucks and rescue cars could not get through, and this increased the demoralization.

Ace drove us around the town, which has a current population of about four thousand. Because of the highway, the government put in an electric plant which now belongs to the town, and there is a quarter-million dollar system of water mains and sewerage. Since there was much rebuilding after the fire, Dawson Creek has modern stores and hotels at the present time.

In one of the vacant lots in the business district, thirty or more sled dogs, powerful creatures—white Siberians with silvery eyes, gray huskies like wolves, and dark Norwegian elkhounds—were chained in a wide semicircle. They had been in the army and were now on their way to Aklavik in the Arctic. They were to be shipped to Fort Nelson by the Alaska Highway, then down the Laird River by boat to the Mackenzie, on the delta of which stands Aklavik. Some of the dogs had been close friends of servicemen; I hoped they would get good treatment and companionship where they were going.

The next day we drove out with the Comstocks to their farm, where Tiny, besides her tractor driving and hunting, had managed to achieve a lovely and flourishing garden. Families drove for many miles to see her flowery borders, for in this new country, as Tiny said, the people had not had time for planting flowers and trees, or painting houses.

Dawson Creek seemed the very edge of the frontier to me; at least it was the only place I had ever been where they offered you Scotch before breakfast instead of tomato juice. But it was too tame for Ace. "Have to get out of town right away," he said. "Out where there's something to see." The Comstocks had made many plans for us, but as we could only stay the week end, we took a two-day trip to Hudson Hope.

This was an outpost of the Hudson's Bay Company far up the solitudes of the Peace River. Lee would not let me see the map before we started. As I have said, many of the main roads in western Canada are gravel and these are marked in solid red lines on the road maps; when I say this road showed merely as a dotted black line I have said enough.

As far as Fort St. John we drove on the Alaska Highway, which was a broad graveled road through rolling hills. Several forest fires raged about on distant hilltops in a vigorous manner, but no one seemed to mind. Where we crossed the Peace River there was a great new bridge, built at the cost of three and a half million dollars to take the place of a ferry which had been the only way to cross. Fifty miles

from a railroad and built under great handicaps of weather and wartime shortages, it was finished in less than seven months.

Of the four great rivers we had encountered, the Assiniboine, the Saskatchewan, the Athabaska, and the Peace, the last belongs to the far north. The whole Peace River area is a plateau with uplands rising above the surrounding country. The river has cut deeply, so that the plateau heights are sometimes eight hundred feet above the stream itself. We gloried in this river of the true wilderness, hardly marred by the habitations of man, with its lovely irregular shorelines usually forested, occasionally broken by bits of meadow or marsh.

The Peace River Block is an area of more than three million acres. "This subregion is included in the Forest Belt," Mackintosh states in *Prairie Settlement*, "although much of the land is parkland or very lightly forested. Indeed it may be considered the last outpost of the grasslands of the interior of this continent." For the Great Plains of Canada are in two drainage districts, one the tremendous Saskatchewan basin which extends to the United States border, the other here where the Mackenzie, Athabaska, and Peace rivers drain the northern plain.

In this Peace River area new settlement has been most active in the last twenty years. Mackintosh says the land-seeker, squatter, homesteader, and settler with capital are still active, villages have sprung up in a few weeks, and "though not necessarily the last agricultural frontier in Canada, the Peace River Country is the largest single area of active settlement. . . . Only in Siberia, where settlement is also pushing northward, does one find similar problems." Not that the Peace River is newly explored; the fur traders knew it before the nineteenth century.

Fort St. John was a lively town. "I always like this trip," Ace said. "Something's always happening in this country." I noticed that though he spoke with pride of the prosperity of the region, the grains and fruits, the healthy livestock and the modern services which were being introduced, it was the adventure in the land which had the great appeal for him.

Now he showed us the airport, the third largest in Canada, and took us in to the Husky Cafe to meet Mrs. Carroll, otherwise Sammy, who had driven her dog sled from the Skeena River to New York City; after which we went to the newspaper office to see Mrs. Margaret Murray, the energetic editor of the *Alaska Highway News*.

This brisk weekly has current events and pertinent facts to offer, but it is the neighborly items which give it special flavor.

> The six feet and 200 pounds of Bruce Peck came near being a casualty awhile ago when he approached a big buck deer he thought was very dead. The deer jumped up and made a terrific slash at him, sending his rifle flying in the bush and ripping open his whole clothing.
>
> Gary Powell ran into timber wolves that had just killed a deer last week. He opened up and shot three of them dead as a dodo. Having no more shells he called it a day. A good day too, eh Gary? Should have a snort of rum on that—
>
> Mr. Holden used this building as a hog shed when the price of hogs was satisfactory. Now Mr. Holden thinks there is more money in the Pool business. . . . So he remodelled this building. Let's hope the hog perfume evaporates before we start playing pool.
>
> Since Smiths moved to town they have had plenty of trouble. When anybody comes to town they bring their dog along. While the people do their shopping the dogs feast on Mrs. Smith's chickens and eggs. Too bad Mrs. Smith can't shoot. Better take lessons, Mrs. Smith.

Near Fort St. John was the Wilde and Lawless outfit, which seemed to me a name almost too flamboyant to be chosen even here. But Mr. Wilde and Mr. Lawless were actualities, big-game guides, who had chanced to become partners and were preparing a Wilde and Lawless Stampede for the fall.

The sixty-five miles from Fort St. John to Hudson Hope were beautiful and terrifying. When we had left the mountain roads behind us

I had secretly breathed a gentle sigh of relief. But they had been carefully kept; now, after we turned off the Alaska Highway, there was
a one-track lane, ungraveled, so that in bad weather it was exceedingly
slippery and treacherous. I don't know what you were supposed to
do if cars ever came from the other direction, though luckily none
appeared.

It was a roller coaster road with no guard rail, though Tiny said,
"It's all right if it just doesn't rain." As we climbed one steep curve
with a sheer drop to the valley on its outer rim Ace said casually,
"Last time here it was so slick we had to back down and start over
three times." My toes curled and shivered.

But actually the rickety road only added to the untamed landscape,
the great hills, and the valley through which the glorious river came
down from the snow peaks far on our horizon, winding through
the spruce and pine forests, with many islands breaking its course.

Bear Flats was a post office, though no town was visible. We
stopped there to meet an old-timer who had moved in long ago;
he had come down the Peace River by boat, which was the only way
to get into this country until this road was sketched out. We went

into a farmhouse to visit Mrs. Dopp, its hostess. She had come face to face not long before with a bear who was climbing in her pantry window. She had shot at it, but as she was understandably excited, her shots had gone wild and drilled the floor and the wall. Slightly impatient at this, her husband took the gun away from her, and now she had to frighten bears away by beating on her dishpan with a potato masher. "I'm so silly," she said deprecatingly. "I think I see bears all over the barnyard when it's getting dark."

Our road grew more impetuous. One short cut was such a reckless one that Tiny would hardly let Ace drive down it and he had to promise he would take the long way coming back. After hitting the main trail again I said to Ace, "You don't know what a compliment I paid your driving, not squeaking or gasping on that road." "Maybe," he said, "but I noticed you were ridin' pretty high-rumped for a while."

Next we stopped at a ranch along the river, where an Englishman, John Ardill, raised thoroughbred cattle and horses. It was a beautifully kept place and the ranch house was unusually attractive with paintings and heirlooms which his wife had brought from her home in Holland. This was a close-knit family; the grown children, cultured and intelligent, had been home-educated. The three sons worked on the ranch and the daughter, now in her twenties, had, besides helping in the house, the task of breaking the high-spirited horses. We had afternoon tea on the long porch, and Mr. Ardill showed us the pelts of two wolves he had killed on the range. They were superb, more than seven feet long, one a gray that was almost white and one very dark.

After Half Way River, which is a jumping-off place for hunting parties, we came to a little log house with flowers around it and a big corral near by. The Rutledges lived here.

Leo Rutledge was a fine type of Northerner, who farmed in the summer, trapped through the winter, and took big-game hunters out with his pack trains in the fall. His attractive wife, Ethel, had come over from England when she was a girl, and when she heard that an

171

invalid woman in far-off Hudson Hope wanted a companion, she came here, having a lively curiosity about this remote north country. She met Leo and in a few months they were married.

Now they had three children, and we took a special fancy to the oldest, Valerie, who was thirteen. Valerie was a darling. She had a look of flyaway delicacy, but she wrangled horses for her father in the hunting season and took pack trains by herself for miles into the mountains to meet him.

The summer before, she had had a chance to go to school for a short time at Hudson Hope, and every Friday afternoon she walked the ten miles alone through the uninhabited region to get home for the week end. Then on Monday morning she walked back. Sometimes she saw bear, and once a moose followed her for a long time.

This year she was taking first-year high-school work by correspondence. Every day she took a path up the hill to a deserted cabin where she spent long hours studying alone. That zigzag little path seemed to me very touching.

Leo was an expert on the big game of the region. He said that the moose went up above timberline in the hunting season but came down to the valley in winter (it is milder here, only twenty to fifty below in sheltered spots) and were hard on the fences. The bears were everywhere this year, he told us; he had never seen so many. Neither had we, for that matter. As there is no closed season on them, he usually kills one in early September "to see if they are getting any lard on them," and then takes the hunters out on their trail. Mountain sheep are found on rock slides, though there were few of them around this year, possibly because of the wolves.

Leo liked the reproduction of a painting Lee had made of two wolves. "What I don't see is how you could get that typical winter 'bloom' on them," he said. "I'd imagine that even if you did have a model, a wolf in captivity would not have a natural appearance."

"I used to see them in Minnesota," Lee answered, "though not often."

"I've seen as many as twenty-five in a day," Leo told him. "One day a hunter and I spent almost a whole day on a mountainside, watching fifteen on a high knoll. They were out of range for shooting and were in a position where we had to let them make the first move. In the evening we managed to get within twenty feet of two white ones, but the hunter only blew some fur off. They did not give us a chance at another shot."

Afterwards I realized that we hadn't asked Leo about grizzlies, and I regretted that. I have been told it is now one of the rarest of American big game, has vanished from much of its range, and continues to retreat from the hunters' rifles.

This was grizzly country, as *Manitoba and the Great North West* reports. "Peace River is however the home of the bear, as within the Rocky Mountains the terrible grizzly makes his habitation. Grizzlies were never hunted by the Beaver Indians except in revenge for the death or maiming of a friend, and then it was done as a matter of duty. The size of their feet and the length of their claws make them terrible to encounter, as one blow from such an animal would tear a man almost to pieces."

After we said good-by to the Rutledges, our road to Hudson Hope became even narrower; in places it looked as if someone had ploughed one furrow in the shifting shale. Tiny, who was used to traveling over it, kept a newspaper to read on certain stretches, so that she needn't look down or ahead.

The people here take this road as high adventure and never think of staying home because of adverse weather. One driver had lost a leg and since he could not stop his car without great difficulty, his solution was to drive twice as fast as anyone else, so that the trip wouldn't last long, whatever happened.

The small post of Hudson Hope, standing in deep forest on the irregular rocky curve of the river, below the canyon, struck me as one of the most unusual little places I had ever seen. It was tiny, just a stepping-off stone for hunters and trappers. The latter follow trap lines which are sometimes a hundred miles long, through sub-zero winter weather which may reach sixty below.

The village consisted of a Hudson's Bay Company store, a small hotel, a grocery store, and tiny post office. The few log houses were scattered through the woods in a haphazard way and the smallest possible Church of England chapel (made of logs, with gothic windows and an altar cloth embroidered with wild roses) was quaint and delightful.

The simple hotel once housed Charles Bedeaux, that fabulous international character who loaned his French chateau to the Duke and Duchess of Windsor when they were married. He made millions by suspected means, became a friend of Hitler and Franco, and committed suicide when the United States charged him with treason. In 1934, when he took a fancy to prove that it was possible to get from Fort St. John to the Alaskan Coast over the Rockies, he stopped here.

He had an extravagant pack train, motor trucks, special French cars

174

built by Citroen, more than a hundred horses, caviar, champagne, and folding bathtubs. The expedition, which finally turned back two hundred miles from the coast after the trucks gave out and the horses developed hoof rot from the muskeg trails, was reported to have cost half a million dollars.

At Hudson Hope this expensive outfit and forty-seven people were held idle for half a day, because Bedaux disapproved of the way a picture in the dining room was framed and insisted on going into the

woods, getting birchbark, cutting and soaking it, and reframing the picture.

The hotel was being repaired, and the Comstock's room had no door. In ours the window was so high we could not see out, though the fragrance of wild roses and the scent of young balm of Gilead leaves came in. After dinner we walked down to the river and looked up toward the canyon where dinosaur tracks are found on the sloping rocks; sixty million years ago the great reptiles slithered through shallow swamps in countless numbers. We drank the water of the Peace, for Tiny said if we did that we were sure to come again.

We arose at four in the morning. I thought Ace was joking when he suggested it, but if we meant to reach Dawson Creek that night we had to see the Peace River Canyon before breakfast. The sky was bright with dawn when we came sleepily out of the hotel, to find coffee ready for us, made on Tiny's Sterno heater which perched cheerfully on a lumber pile by the half-built hotel porch.

After the hot strong coffee it was wonderful to see the Peace River Canyon in the early dawn—though our road was so primitive we could hardly find it at times. But men were trucking out coal from "glory holes" along the river, for this country, besides having an abundance of fur-bearing animals, has great potential mineral wealth and geologists say that three billion tons of coal are available.

We drove through enormous and ancient aspens and reached the gorge where the powerful river abruptly narrowed to a channel less than two hundred feet across. Massive slabs of rock walled it in and huge logs which had washed down from the rainy belt, where trees grow so recklessly, lay in gigantic piles of driftwood. In about nine miles the river drops two hundred and fifty feet and it is estimated that five million horsepower can be developed here.

But I would far rather have it remain as it is, a lonely forest where green-shadowed cliffs are washed by the wild river and the smooth dangerous swell of the suddenly imprisoned torrent breaks into foaming rapids. The silence here was broken only by the song of a distant thrush. That is what I will always remember.

Our way back was filled with warm sunlight. Very different from the last time they were there, Ace said, which was in wintertime. He had met a man whose big nose was frozen white. "Why, man," he called, "your nose is frozen." "It is, is it?" said the man; "The big buzzard is always a-doing that!"

At the edge of Hudson Hope we stopped at the trapper cabin of

Jean Boring. In the yard was a baby moose, a very small one. He was as fuzzy as a baby chicken and his head came out of his shoulders as if he had no neck at all. His long legs seemed to take him places in spite of himself, he had appealingly long eyelashes; altogether he was an irresistible infant. We liked him even before we heard his tragic little history.

A few days before, Jean said, he heard a commotion across the river and went over in his boat. He found a battle royal going on between a great black bear and a cow moose. As her calf was only a few hours old and could not run away, the mother circled round and round him, keeping between him and the bear, while she struck at her enemy with her hoofs. The bear would bide his time until she turned a trifle and then slash at her flank.

Jean said, "It was a mess when I got there. Blood all over; both the moose and the bear were dripping. Turned out, she marked him as much as he did her."

Jean shot the bear. But the moose was so badly torn that she could

not rally. She did not even have the strength to look at her calf, she simply stood there with her head hanging and Jean had to shoot her too.

When he started back to the river, the little moose followed. So Jean just put him in the boat and took him home.

"What a lot of interesting people we met," I said on our way back to Dawson Creek.

"Finest people in the world in this country," Ace said proudly. "The longer you know them the better they are. The weak die off and the cowards don't come."

13.

Buffalo on Our Road

THE American bison dates back to the Middle Pleistocene period, four hundred thousand years ago. He is supposed to have wandered over from Asia, across a problematic land bridge or across ice. At that time there were several species, one of which, the long-horned, had horns with the tremendous spread of six feet.

The first written record comes from 1521, when Cortez saw a captive bison in Montezuma's zoo. Three kinds, the plains, mountain, and woods buffalo, are mentioned by early explorers, but all three seem to be the same species. The slight difference in appearance can be attributed to environment. The woods was the largest and finest; the mountain, which often climbed to timberline, had thick strong legs and a lighter, shorter body.

The animals are not true buffalo, as the water buffalo are. The French first called them *les boeufs*, which the English pronounced buffle and later buffalo. These bison are gregarious creatures, and many small bands of them combined to form the tremendous herds which made them famous.

They formerly ranged as far east as western New York and Pennsylvania, and south to the border of Georgia. But the vast multitudes were west of the Mississippi and extended down into Mexico and up to Great Slave Lake. Estimates which claim to be conservative place the numbers at sixty million, when the white men began to move west. There are records of hordes that extended twenty-five by fifty miles, and one hunter killed as many as three thousand in a season.

The buffalo had always been addicted to dying in great numbers. Because of their habit of moving en masse, herds of them would get bogged down in mud and be unable to escape. Or in wintertime they would plunge into deep snow in the coulees and stick there until they starved to death. The Indians too would drive them in panic-stricken flight over the cliffs and hundreds would be killed.

The buffalo took those catastrophes in his stride. But we easily exterminated him. The ugly story has been told so often that I would like to turn away from it, but we should not forget what happened.

From the advent of the first explorers, the bison were killed in incredible numbers. The supply seemed endless. During the Civil War, Col. Charles Goodnight wrote of the southern herds, "When for some reason the herd became excited it was very dangerous. . . . As far as the eye could see, north, south and west . . . the whole country was covered with what appeared to be a monstrous moving brown blanket, the length and breadth of which could not be determined. The number of animals it contained was beyond the human mind to estimate."

The Plains Indians lived on the buffalo. He was food for them, shelter and clothing. They used his hide for robes, bedding, moccasins, leggings, shirts, lodge covering, and round bull boats. The tough skin on the neck was made into war shields and the ribs used as runners for dog sleds. Hoofs made glue, the stomach lining made water buckets, the horns were carved into spoons and sometimes bows, which were rarities and greatly prized.

But after the Civil War the railroads began to push across the western plains; and to get rid of the buffalo, professional hunters were brought in. The extermination of the bison began. The Indians protested, but the government made no attempt to stop the slaughter of the animals on which the existence of the tribes depended. In fact, the Secretary of the Interior stated that he would rejoice when the last buffalo was gone as far as the Indian question was concerned. The Representative from Illinois introduced a bill for the protection of the buffalo, saying that he was not in favor of civilizing the Indian by starving him to death. But the bill was pigeonholed, and the bloody destruction went on. Usually the dead animals lay and rotted, with no attempt at salvaging meat or hide. Sometimes the tongues were saved; they sold at twenty-five cents apiece.

After the trains began to run, they would sometimes have to wait hours if a herd decided to cross the tracks. Engineers tried charging the herd, but they only derailed their engines. Passengers would shoot for sport from the windows of the coaches. A Santa Fe conductor remarked caustically that in the early 70's one could have walked a hundred miles along the right of way without once stepping off the carcases of slaughtered bison.

The southern herds were annihilated first. In 1880, the ruin of the northern animals, finer than those of the south, began. Then the Northern Pacific extended its line west from Bismarck, in spite of the solemn treaty the United States Government had made with the Indians, giving them the country "as long as grass grew and water ran." The Indians were ordered to a reservation in South Dakota where there was little game, and this was when they attacked Custer's command.

In 1880 the buffalo swarmed on this range in countless numbers. Their last year was in 1883. Then a gigantic herd, between fifty and eighty thousand, crossed the Yellowstone to go north over the Canadian border. Almost all were killed by hide-hunters before they reached the boundary.

Garretson, in *The American Bison*, says, "from that month (November) the wild American Bison was practically a thing of the past. The barbarous brutality practised in the final slaughter is almost beyond belief. The hunters kept fires blazing all night along the river banks and guarded every water hole, knowing that sooner or later the thirst-tortured creatures would be driven, in a desperate effort to slake their thirst, to face the deadly rifles of the hunters, which ceased only when there was nothing more to shoot."

By 1900 not a single wild buffalo was left on the Great Plains. There were some woods buffalo at Great Slave Lake, and a very few plains buffalo on the upper Peace River.

There was one large herd remaining on the whole continent. This was in Montana where two ranchers had brought about forty buffalo from Kansas and from Manitoba. These increased to three hundred, and as some of them were sold, they became the beginnings of small herds about the United States. In 1906, seven hundred were purchased by Canada and forty-eight of these were the nucleus of the numbers now in Elk Island National Park. This park now boasts the finest herd of bison in Canada. It has steadily increased, being free from the diseases which attack the animals in other regions, and now numbers more than a thousand.

The park is in Alberta, twenty-five miles east of Edmonton, and we wanted to visit it. Coming down from Dawson Creek, Lee had planned for us to stop over in Edmonton and drive out from there, but Edmonton's hotels were crowded to the eaves. So we drove in a drenching rain to the park, and decided to stay all night at Lamont, a small town north of the preserve.

Elk Island Park is in the rolling country known as the Beaver Hills, on the border between forest and open plain. It was established in 1906 as a preserve for elk, the last wild herd of the region being in danger of extinction; in 1922 it was increased to fifty square miles, and is now unique by reason of its bison.

The road into the park looked tempting, in spite of the rain, for in preparation for the summer tourists it had been newly graded. But the repairing had been done so recently that the road was a very shifting one, with shoulders as soft as butter.

We drove from the south entrance to the north one, through woods,

by lakes and ponds, passing the meadows of wild hay on which the buffalo feed. But not until we got nearly to the north gate did we see buffalo. Then we caught sight of several bulls wandering about freely in a clearing.

They were different from any bison I had ever seen. The ones I had watched had been dusty unkempt creatures, looking too weary to carry their great heads. But these were sturdy, vital creatures, compact with energy. Their coats were unusually dark and thick, their manes were great curling masses. They were most magnificent specimens.

As we watched them, one huge old fellow perched above our road on a cut bank; suddenly he plunged down, galloped in front of us, full of vigor, and shot up the bank in a lithe, swift fashion amazing in such a massive creature.

These bison are our largest game animal. A bull may stand six feet at the shoulder and weight up to two thousand pounds. The head is very wide, with small curved horns and a great beard like a patriarch's; a thick mane enlarges the shoulders and hump to huge proportions, then the body slopes off into small hindquarters and the tail is a mere wisp. The shoulder hump is formed by a prolongation of the dorsal vertebrae, which reaches its height at the shoulders and then drops straight down into the neck, so that the head hangs very low.

A younger bull appeared, and his uptilted horns gave him a water buffalo look. He still had patches of shedding hair, though it was late for that. The buffalo sheds in the spring and for a time becomes almost naked, except on head, hump, and forelegs.

At the north gate we found the road to Lamont was too slippery to drive on; an army jeep had just barely got through. We started back to the park headquarters to ask advice, slowed down to look at a buffalo wallowing in a marsh, and skidded into a ditch.

I stayed in the car while Lee went for help, and watched the solitary buffalo. He seemed to be eating marsh grass. Bison diet is sometimes quite varied; the ability of buffalo to survive on snow-covered range, for instance, is greater than that of domestic cattle.

Of course, when they were on the plains the buffalo grass was their principal food. This was a short grass which grew in curly tufts. It is one of the most valuable of pasture grasses, as it stands heat and cold, trampling, and drought. Before the settlers came, much of the prairie was covered with it and the whole country was said to look like a clipped lawn, weedless until civilization appeared. Now the buffalo grass, crowded out by bluejoint, is found only in small patches.

Lee came back with a park truck, which hauled us out on the road again. We found there was no place for us to stay overnight except a tent, on the edge of a ravine in deep woods. We gladly accepted that; it had a floor, which we appreciated especially since the rain was falling in torrents.

After dinner it cleared for a time and we drove to the entrance gate and back. Buffalo wandered through the varying meadows of grass, muskeg, and underbrush. We saw one old bull couched like a sultan in a poplar thicket that glittered with goldfinches and bluebirds. He even had a brilliant oriole instead of a nightingale to sing to him.

At one small lake with black terns flying over yellow waterlilies, two

184

moose came down the hillside as we passed. On another hill we saw a line of bison against the sky. Their heads swung low, their knickers bulged above their tiny feet, their big beards waggled wildly as they paced across the hill.

They have various gaits: the pace, a trot, and a gallop. When they are in a hurry they pitch in heavy fashion, but their speed is surprising. They do not move like cattle, but spread their hind feet apart as a horse does. When the buffalo is going at full speed, his hind feet come up in front of his forefeet, almost on either side of his nose.

When bison graze they scatter out, but on migration—they are migratory animals—they travel in single file, and their trails are worn deep in the earth. The buffalo invariably follows the line of least resistance, and is an incomparable engineer. His paths were often followed by the early surveyors.

Back at Astotin Lake, we left the car near our tent and took a walk along the shore of the lake, which is an irregular body of water, more than two miles long, with many islands.

Twilight peace was around us. We sat down by a sandy point and ducks drifted about us in contented pairs on vaguely rippled water. Across the narrow bay a long footbridge led to an island and on its railing sat, of all things, a row of buffleheads. Feet wide apart, there they sat as if it were the most natural thing in the world for fat little ducks to be perching birds. A beaver had wrecked a small dock and was towing portions home. It became interested in Lee, and I thought meant to gnaw him down and add him to the beaver house.

We went back to our tent in the dark. When we had accepted it, I had thought I might worry about buffalo wandering in the night (we once had a moose almost blunder on our camp) but they never entered my head, let alone the tent. I felt lulled and contented, with the rain loud on our slanting roof and tiny poplar leaves twirling against dim sky outside our open tent flap.

Phoebes singing woke us to a bright June morning. Fragrance was strong in the damp air, and we stepped out on a carpet almost too delicately ornate with twinflowers, bluebells, and wild roses. Bird songs rose around us in a confusion of melody.

As we went down to breakfast at the club we passed three moose by a lake and a small party of buffalo splashing down a trail, the early sunlight making halos around their shaggy heads.

We stopped by one pond to watch a Holboell's grebe building her nest in a perfectly hopeless spot. Most of the grebes had built up little islands in quiet water, but she had chosen a site where the current swept her material away as soon as she placed it. With great industry and no common sense, however, she kept lugging large bundles up from the lake bottom, showing them to her mate, and dropping them on the ill-chosen spot. Sometimes her burden dripped down over her head like a widow's veil, sometimes it trailed far behind her. Her mate took a perfunctory interest in the first loads, but you could tell he was bored with her preoccupation and soon he went to sleep.

After breakfast we went across a rustic bridge to a high island. Terns still fluttered, and the blue ripples were studded with buffleheads. The little black-and-white wildfowl were everywhere. A large colony of grebes was about too. On the island itself we found the lovely satiny waxwings in the pines, their crests erect and gay—both the cedar, and the larger Bohemian waxwing, which was a new bird for me.

Out beyond the island a tremendous splashing led us to investigate. Two female goldeneyes were fighting over a large flock of tiny ducklings. Was one trying to kidnap the children? We finally decided, since the ducklings came in two sizes, that both broods had mingled and the mothers could not get them separated.

It was sad and funny. The ducklings, with black caps pulled down over their little eyes and two large white spots, like buttons, on each of their little behinds, looked like rowdy urchins. But they were the fond mothers' prides and joys and neither hen was willing to give up a single one of her darlings.

The two females fought on and on. One would herd the ducklings off as fast as she could, then the other would make a sneak, with the front half of her body underwater and her head and neck stretched out flat on the surface. She would dash at her rival and there would be, if not bloodshed, at least plenty of watershed, all about.

The two fought till they were completely exhausted. They would lie panting on the water and then start in fighting all over again. The innocent ducklings drifted about, completely confused as to whom they should follow or what was their bounden duty.

Finally one hen went swimming off triumphant, with seven youngsters in her wake, four big and three small. The other female complacently rounded up the remaining flock and peace settled down upon the lake.

It was time to leave the preserve, for we were to drive eastward again across the prairie provinces. By the northern highway this time, instead of the southern one. Through the park, roadways were still

187

wet and treacherous from the rain, and Sunday cars began to meet us in the worst possible places.

We were driving downhill when a herd of buffalo ambled across the road, and as we stopped to let them go by, the car went in the ditch again. It was incongruous in the extreme to sit there immovably and see these contemporaries of the mastodon and the woolly mammoth stroll by in the sunlight.

Big bulls came in front, their massive heads a rich brown in the sun; then came the cows; and last of all five babies ran along. The calves are born in May, so these were less than a month old. They looked like small domestic calves; the characteristic buffalo hump did not show as yet, but they carried their heads low, as their noble leaders did.

Sometimes they skipped and kicked sidewise, sometimes they shoved each other, but they followed the line. A bison calf is a sturdy little thing, and is able to follow the herd like this within a few hours of birth, which of course was a necessity in the prairie days when wolves and coyotes were an ever-present danger.

I wondered if the buffalo ever resented their visitors. I would have hated for them to resent us actively, for even with the car I did not feel we were their equal in combat. Though when they fight among themselves, at least, they do not rush head-on, as has been reported, but use their tremendous strength to push each other around, then plunge their horns into an unprotected flank. When they were pursued by man in the early days, they usually fled, but a bull might stop without warning, pivot on his forefeet and swing his hindquarters around, then charge his pursuer.

Writers seem to differ widely about the buffalo's character. One says he is most intelligent, another that he is sluggish, mild, and slow to learn by experience, while still a third insists that he has a one-track mind and whatever he does, he does with all his might. Hornaday writes that the buffalo has steady nerves and a serene temper, and that while the herds on the plains were careless and unsuspicious the last survivors had learned wisdom enough to hide from man in the badlands and mountain valleys. Garretson, however, says that the bison's temper cannot be relied on, at least in captivity, and that it is dangerous to turn one's back on a buffalo. If you confront him and advance, he will surrender; but if you turn around, even for an instant, he will attack.

Feeling personally interested, I asked the park superintendent about this. But it was like asking someone if his family was likely to be murderous and vicious. He said quite firmly that in his eyes the buffalo was the monarch of the plains, a peace-loving animal who had far too much dignity to indulge in treachery. "To protect the right and freedom of himself and his herd," the superintendent said, "when molested or cornered he becomes seventeen or eighteen hundred pounds of fighting fury, and uses his horns and hoof with a speed unbelievable in an animal of such size."

As we drove out the park entrance, Lee said, "There's one thing we missed seeing in the Elk Island National Park."

"There was?" I asked. "What was it?"

"Elk."

14.

Flin Flon

East of Elk Island Park we left the border country between mountain and plain, and came out on prairie again. Wheat fields were interspersed with aspen groves. Prairie sloughs had gay groups of canvasbacks, pintails, bluewings, and mallards. The buffleheads disappeared with the buffalo, but now there were many ruddies. Black terns still swooped, mixed now with the Franklin's gulls so prevalent on the plains.

A small breeze rollicked like a puppy, and we left the car and took a walk with it far across the open prairie. The air had cleared, and beyond the great curve of the earth silver thunderheads stood glorious above horizons. I felt so free, so *sure*! My spirits did not need to rise; they were already high, but they expanded quite explosively.

One slough was in its yellow period. Yellowlegs were wading, yellow-headed blackbirds clung to slim reeds. Low bushes of the silver willow with their exquisite pointed squares of saffron flowers and small yellow buttercups on land matched the baby ducks in the water. Over the golden peas and yellow cinquefoil many marbled godwits were flying, and these beautiful tawny shore birds (whose long bills are upcurved instead of curving downward as the bills of curlew do) were shrieking about us in a fury: "They're crazy, crazy, crazy!"—"Correct! Correct! Correct!" they screamed. These insults were unfair, and deliberate, designed to make us take our injured dignity far away. But I am calmer about such public tirades than I used to be. I know they are due, in part at least, to nervous tension; nests are somewhere about.

Eastward the country grew more and more open, and the stands of aspens, which were the only trees, shrank to brush.

Once more we met the Saskatchewan. This sounds a simple statement of fact, but of all the Canadian rivers we had passed the Saskatchewan, with its great character, its quiet grandeur, had most captured our imagination. Before I saw it the Saskatchewan meant only a song from a romantic musical to me. At Medicine Hat it first became a reality, and then as we met it and left it and met it again so many times, each meeting had a greater impact upon us. Now the name Saskatchewan meant a real personality, a great power in the land.

For the Saskatchewan dominates the prairie provinces. It is to them what the Mississippi is to the middle west. Besides which, as it had been the main artery to the west for the early fur trade, it has a particular appeal historically as well as geographically.

Its waters come from the most diverse and widely separated regions. The South Saskatchewan's tributaries, rising in the Rocky Mountains, are, from south to north: the St. Mary, near the United States boundary; the Belly River, draining part of our Glacier Park; the Waterton River, from the Waterton Lakes Park; Oldman River, coming from the area around Crowsnest Pass; the Bow River, which we met at Banff and Calgary. Then the North Saskatchewan takes over the country. It rises among the glaciers near Mt. Hooker, flows through the northern section of Banff Park, crosses the Columbia Ice Field Highway, passes through Edmonton, and meets the South Branch in the northern part of Saskatchewan Province.

The water that flows in this imposing river is mountain water, snow water; very little is added to the north and south Saskatchewan rivers after they come to the prairies, for the water of Red Deer River, which joins the South Branch after it reaches the plain, also comes from the Rockies, while the Battle, which is the large tributary of the North Branch, rises near Edmonton. After the two great branches join, the Saskatchewan takes its aloof course through the wide prairies until it flows into Lake Winnipeg, and then north, as the Nelson, into the Arctic Ocean.

Following the river, we stayed overnight at the delightful town of Saskatoon, and from our corner turret in the huge chalet owned by the Canadian National we looked down at the great river, which had known such savage wildernesses, at it flowed past formal gardens under arched bridges of stone. But we too have risen rapidly in the world, I said to Lee, one night in a canvas tent and the next in a chateau tower.

On the edge of Saskatoon, just by the Royal Canadian Air Force barracks, there were a number of shallow ponds where we found the greatest concentration of birds we had seen anywhere, even in the Delta marshes, although there was unusually heavy traffic on the roads close by.

The pools were like kaleidescopes. Above the bright blue water, gold-speckled from the early sun, flew wheeling flocks of yellow-headed blackbirds. Red-winged blackbirds swayed on the reeds along the edge, flaunting their scarlet and gold epaulets with brazen pride. Wildfowl swept overhead, and the water itself was crowded with canvasbacks, shovelers, mallards, and baldpates. There were many broods of ducklings intent on getting into everyone's way, and the mother ducks called to them in quiet conversational tones; it took constant quacking to keep a brood together in such a turmoil.

The edges of the ponds were dancing with shore birds, hundreds of them. The great numbers were on migration, not nesting here, for none of them screamed at us when we left the car. Among the killdeer running in quick, light steps, the willets which stood still to lift their flashing black-and-white wings high over their backs, and the sand-

pipers teetering and bowing, was a robin pretending to be a shore
bird too.

Constantly, on our journey, the robin had appeared in the strangest
places—high on mountains, deep in forest, through the muskeg—so
that I had had to revise my idea of it as a suburbanite. But though I
like robins better the farther from civilization I find them, I am not as
susceptible to their charms as I am to those of less popular birds;
English sparrows and screech owls need my affection more. My heart
really went out to this robin among the shore birds, however; she
looked as incongruous as a short housewife trying to be at ease in a
group of long-legged ballet dancers.

We crossed the Saskatchewan that morning on a ferry attached to
a cable so that the current pulled us across. The ferry had a large side-
wheel hand-turned by a tall old blue-eyed man who looked like a sea
captain. He had run the ferry back and forth across this lonely river
for thirty-one years.

East from the Saskatchewan the land was so arid that boys were
hauling water barrels for miles, jolting along with horse and wagon to
isolated farmhouses. It was an alkali region. Here again were lakes

193

pale and dead, while others lay like dim blue shadows with stone-white edges.

It was curlew country, and the exultant calls rang about us as the birds flew by with their long sickle bills clear-cut and their legs trailing behind them. Far over the grass we could see them run along with their wings raised high above their backs. A large flock of marbled godwits, a brilliant orange in the sun, rose to spiral high in an updraft of warm air. As they floated upward in a lifting circle, round and round, they seemed to be fashioned from pure transparent gold.

One advantage in long-time bird watching is that any experience is enriched because of former adventures. Now this sight was welcome both for its own sake and because it brought back to us the memory of the most transcendent of all our birding experiences. This was one spring when Lee and I, with Dr. Breckenridge of the Minnesota Museum of Natural History, had gone to North Platte, Nebraska, to get specimens and background sketches for a sandhill crane group.

I had supposed we would see, if we were lucky, perhaps a hundred of the elegant cranes. These birds, with their pearl-gray plumage and little scarlet caps, are among the largest of our birds, and their wide wings stretch six feet from one tip to the other; they have slim stream-lined bodies and El Greco legs and bills. It is an event to see two or three, but we saw forty thousand.

They were all over the flat landscape, their croaking trills shaking the air like the exultant shouts of creatures landing from another planet. They fed in the stubble of the cornfields and danced their stylized courtship dances, bowing and skipping and twirling in the air, all through the spring meadows.

But the most amazing sight was to see these great flocks spiral up-ward among the snowy thunderheads. On a still sunny day when there were strong updrafts of warm air, the cranes rose in tremendous flocks from the fields. They flew at first in low immense circles, in such dense clouds that there was hardly space between them as their scalloped wings made an allover pattern against the April sky.

Then they flew into the currents of rising air, where they circled round and round and up and up, with set wings. Hundreds close to-gether, they went spiraling high, their wide pinions absolutely motion-less, glittering and darkening as they wheeled.

The lofty circling was swift and steep, and the whirl of air so power-ful that the cranes soared completely out of sight, over a mile, perhaps two miles, in the air. They would disappear into blue infinity and then reappear on the way earthward, in the broken lines which characterized their descent.

We had seen the white ibis spiral upward in the Everglades, and Lee had painted that spectacle; but there we had seen only dozens of birds together, not unbelievable multitudes like the cranes.

So now, in Saskatchewan, the marbled godwits brought that wild thrill to our pulses again. For its own sake, too, the phenomenon was

195

interesting to us. We had not known that shore birds would soar like that.

Crows were learning by personal experience, today, that there was no rest for the wicked. Whenever we saw a crow he was being chased by an irate bird, usually a blackbird but sometimes by a mere dot of righteous indignation. Magpies and crows, both murderous reprobates, took it turn and turn about in harrying each other; whoever it was that happened to be the pursuer always uttering loud cries of disapproval. "If that isn't a case of the pot calling the kettle black!" Lee said.

As it grew later in the afternoon the hot winds became deliciously light and soft. There were occasional creeks now, and we ate a picnic supper by a cattail pond. "Pintail pups," as Lee called them, came swimming after their mother through garlands of snowy waterflowers. The long shadows from the aspen thickets fell across the green wheat fields and made them look, in the level light, like splendid lawns.

After our supper we drove on to Yorktown, with Lee protesting at the poplars which stood along the road and shaded it. "We're penned in; it doesn't seem like the prairie," he complained.

Now we deserted our car to take another train ride. We were going north to Flin Flon. It had always been our ambition to go by train to the real tundra, through the woodland caribou country to Churchill on Hudson Bay, and we had hoped this year that the passenger train might have resumed its once-a-week schedule. But there was just one excursion to Churchill this summer, and it was not in June.

So we decided we would at least go up to Flin Flon, six hundred miles north of Winnipeg on the Saskatchewan-Manitoba border, and see what that northern country was like.

Our train went west of Lake Winnipegosis, which is northwest of Lake Manitoba. It soon came to spruce, tamarack, and muskeg, and went north all night. In the morning we were at The Pas, which name had always had a fascination for me. It was at first *Le Pas*, the pass into the northland; later the *Le* was changed to English. A motor road ran as far as The Pas, but north of that there was no way to drive on to Flin Flon.

The train went through lake country. Here was granite rock, the western edge of the great Laurentian Shield, as the canoe country on the borders of Minnesota and Ontario is the southern edge. The forest had not the same beautiful diversity, however, for as one goes north more and more species of trees drop out.

But for many miles along the track the yellow moccasin flowers grew in enormous numbers through the muskeg. To see orchids as plentiful as buttercups and daisies was not unpleasant. The scarlet lilies were extraordinarily large and spring flowers, even the earliest, the marsh marigolds, were mingled with gentians, harebells, and fireweed.

Cranberry Portage, the junction east of Flin Flon, had rocky ledges forested with jackpines and tamarack. Stony shoulders reared up out of muskeg and little black streams ran through bogs of peat. "Oh *look* at them," I exclaimed, so fervently that Lee jumped, thinking I must have seen moose or grizzlies.

197

"It's the dark water," I explained. "After all the pale streams we've seen—white waterfalls, gray glacier rivers, dim alkali ponds, azure mountain lakes, milky torrents—I'm just glad to see dark water again!"

We came to cliffs of pinkish granite. Loons appeared. There were rocky shores to all the lakes now, and high islands spired with spruce. We stopped at Athapap on Lake Athapapuskow, which struck me as an even more unusual address than Skookumchuck. And then came Flin Flon.

"I wonder why Flin Flon," I said casually to Lee, and the porter overheard me. "Just a minute," he said proudly, bringing me a cherished and well-worn newspaper clipping.

This told about Tom Creighton and his party, who first discovered the hidden wealth in the region. They had had with them a dime novel, *The Sunless City*, which told about Joseph Flintabatty Flontain of the Society for the Exploration of Unexplored Regions. One fine day he had found himself in a strange underground region surrounded by mountains of gold and could think of nothing better to do than to escape from it by means of an extinct volcano. When Creighton's party discovered ore in this country, they happened to notice a conical hole leading down into the earth, which looked as if Flintabatty Flontain might have climbed up from it and so they named the place Flin Flon.

Flin Flon was a great disappointment to me. It is a remarkable place, I admit, this huge mining plant in the midst of a vast wilderness. As recently as 1928 Flin Flon consisted only of a few log huts. But as an investigation of the ore deposits showed there were sixteen million tons within the first nine hundred feet, and later even larger ore bodies were found, this was encouraging enough so that an initial outlay of one hundred and twenty-seven million dollars was spent here, before one single ton of ore was sent out. Now the town has a population of ten thousand.

But the name Flin Flon had had such a gay comic-opera sound, and the place seemed to me so far from gay. It was a hot and dusty town, built on hard rock. High in the air the smelter smokestacks and the mine shaft heads, like tall bright-red elevators, rose dramatically, but the rest of the town sprawled in stark ugliness up and down the barren hills.

The streets were narrow, the roads flinty and dusty, and there were only occasional sidewalks though they were badly needed. Wooden stairways led up steep hills, for the town dips and climbs, with levels that vary as much as two hundred and fifty feet.

We tried to explore, but it was hard work. We climbed steep steps and trudged along stony paths. Flin Flon stands on solid rock, and only part of the town has water and sewerage. Even there, as any hole has to be blasted, the pipes cannot run underground. They run on the surface, up and down the hills, boxed in by planks and insulated against freezing. The rest of the town has water delivered by the pail.

But there is electric power and a telephone system, though as no holes can be dug, the telephone poles are held erect by piles of rocks. Some of the small houses were modern and up-to-date. The general effect, however, was meager and drab, except for the gigantic industrial units. Lee wanted to take pictures of the smelters, so we followed a road past them, slipping and stumbling on sharp rocks. I felt totally unmoved by the fact that one of the great buildings was a copper smelter, another a zinc reclaiming plant.

Here are some of Canada's most important producing mines, owned by the Hudson Bay Mining and Smelting Company. The ore is copper and zinc with some silver and gold, and smaller amounts of cadmium, selenium, and tellurium. The capacity of both open-pit and sublevel mining here is over six thousand tons of ore each day.

Such wealth! And yet there wasn't a pleasant place where a stranger could sit down in the whole town. The few restaurants had atmosphere, to be sure, and the one where we had lunch was trying hard for charm. It had signs which admonished "KEEP YOUR FEET DOWN PLEASE," and "NO ROISTERING OR OBSCENE LANGUAGE."

199

After lunch we tried to walk out into the country. There are no motor roads leading from outside into Flin Flon, but there are two short stretches from the town, one of which goes fifteen miles to Beaver Lake, and the other to Phantom Lake, all of two miles away. These are the only drives it is possible to take, and yet there are pleasure cars in Flin Flon.

We wandered out past the mines into a region of knobby hills. Somewhere our train, on our way into town, had passed a lake, but we couldn't find it. To make the steep grade into Flin Flon the railroad swings around in a long loop and this had confused us in our directions, the more so as the sun was obscured. There were heaps of waste rock everywhere, and burned pines stood stiff on distant hills. The town looked burned-over too, with ranks of bare poles that were stuck up for radio aerials.

We sat down on a rock ledge, but there were broken beer bottles and dead brush all around. Lee looked at my expression and laughed. "Forlorn in Flin Flon," he said. I laughed too, but not convincingly, he told me.

The sky was threatening now. Lee clambered up a stony slope littered with stunted poplars, and I followed through the sparse vegetation. When Lee climbed higher, to take photographs of the shaft heads dominating the town, I lay down and gave myself up to despair.

I wondered vaguely why I was so unhappy. After all, not liking a place was no reason for such complete dejection. I am accustomed to feeling depressed at the destruction and distortion of natural beauty through mankind's tireless endeavor. That is a perfectly normal reaction. But this infelicity was far down below the thought level.

Perhaps the weather of my spirit had been too unchangingly sunny or too highly charged with enthusiasm, I thought, and now I was feeling a reversal? But no, I had felt that change of wind at Banff when I had had too much mountain glory. This was a different thing. This was a low-pressure area which I couldn't account for.

All at once I realized what was the matter. I was homesick. That was it. I wanted "my home, my home," as my little niece used to wail when she went visiting.

I enjoyed later an article in the *Saturday Review of Literature* called "Some Notes on Nostalgia," by Beardsley Ruml. It was more or less a defence of homesickness, and insisted that it is as much a reality as are egoic emotions and is an equally significant foundation for behavior. Nostalgic emotion is associated with transformations of the patterns of our outer world as opposed to egoic emotions which are concerned with changes in the patterns of our inner world, Mr. Ruml said, and "in extreme form the symptoms of nostalgia are acute and violent." Mine were, that afternoon.

But after a little I turned over and lifted my head. Above me grass stems were sharply cut against gray whorls of cloud. Grass heads were swaying in the wind. An ant walked sedately, upside down, along one slender stalk.

Why, this was a familiar sight; this was not alien. Grass stems and ants—I had seen them all my life; they were beloved bits of transient homes Lee and I had had, campsites and cabins, picnic places. Affection for these scraps and trifles suddenly warmed me; as long as they were about, I was not lost. I felt at ease. At peace. At home.

When a nature-lover is in an ethereal dream, it is disconcerting to be brought back to facts by a small, practical annoyance. I was shaken from my reverie when a more obscure ant suddenly bit me. But in spite of that, when Lee came back to my hollow, he was relieved to find me looking quite agreeable.

It rained on our way back to town, but I didn't mind. It was surprising what different things I noticed about Flin Flon. Small squares of green lawn, scrupulously tended, and flowering bushes planted along a fence; a hospital on the hill, run by the Gray Nuns of St. Hyacinth; children hilarious in a rocky playground. I even enjoyed our evening meal; no one disobeyed the signs and somebody played a guitar with much abandon in the booth next to us.

Our train left at twilight. The last sight of Flin Flon was a striking one. Scarlet shaft heads towered up against wild storm clouds, and as we circled past the steel-gray lake, the stark houses which stood on its stony shores had lighted windows, little squares of bright gold in the dusk.

"Isn't that a stunning picture," I said to Lee.

"Did you notice the small pond of red mud?" a woman across the aisle inquired. "That's worth millions of dollars. It's full of gold and copper and zinc, if there was just some way to get them out."

"You must live here," I said.

"Yes, I do," she replied, "but I'm going outside for a while. The doctors advise every man, woman, and child to get out of Flin Flon at least once a year. It's too nerve-racking to stay longer, because there's no way to vary the monotony here. I expect you found out it's hard to take even a short walk."

"What about your lakes—Phantom Lake, and Beaver?"

"Phantom does have a beach," she said, "but it's so crowded I don't often go, and the road to Beaver is so rough that I get carsick on it. But we're going to have roads," she added proudly. "Saskatchewan is making plans for a highway here, and Manitoba already has a survey for a road from The Pas."

"What do you do for amusement?" I asked.

"Why, what people do any place," she answered. "There are clubs and organizations, hockey, curling, and of course there's great hunting and fishing. We have a golf course, too, built on the bed of a lake they had to drain. People like to have gardens here, but they're terribly expensive because all the soil has to be bought and shipped in."

"I do enjoy getting outside," she went on. "Last time we went out I heard a youngster say to his mother, 'Mummy, is it a new world?'"

"It must be hard to come back," I said sympathetically.

"Oh, *no*," she replied with surprise. "We all want to come back. The people here are grand, and that's what really makes a place, isn't it?"

I was ashamed that I had felt pity. I remembered bits from Stevenson. "The ground of a man's joy is often hard to hit. . . . We shall see the trunk from which he draws his nourishment, but he himself is above and abroad in the green dome of foliage, hummed through by winds and nested in by nightingales. . . . And the true realism always and everywhere is that of the poets; to find out where joy resides and give it a voice far beyond singing. For to miss the joy is to miss all."

15.

Delta in June

Back in our car again, we headed for Delta. It was like going home. As we went through Manitoba the trees became lofty and more abundant. It was a delight to see the "bluffs" again, and trailing willow boughs taking the place of stunted willow bushes. By the time we reached Dauphin, the maples and elms and oaks looked immeasurably luxuriant in their summer foliage.

We stopped overnight on Riding Mountain, taking it for granted we would see the herds of elk again. Lee wanted to find out how the bulls' horns were progressing, and I intended to see one small calf at least. Of the great numbers we knew were there, however, we had a fleeting glimpse of one lone cow, far back in dark forest.

But that was a small matter. The Manitoba marsh was waiting for us. And how my viewpoint had changed, I marveled, as we neared Portage la Prairie; what a different angle from my first approach to it! Now I was thinking of the region as actually *southern*, way down by the border, United States way. And we seemed only a step or two from the Atlantic, on the eastern edge of the prairie provinces as we were! While the Assiniboine was not unknown and strange, but a cherished companion, the first river we had encountered in Canada.

And Portage itself. How could I ever have considered it a small place? I was overcome with its shining chromium and glass, its traffic, the exotic luxuries, like watermelons, that glittered from shop windows. Portage la Prairie had *both* the great railroads; the Canadian Pacific and the Canadian National stations stood only a few rods apart. All the proud trains that set out from the east to serve the entire Northwest came through Portage before they took the many-fingered tracks that spread out to end of steel at Churchill, Flin Flon, Waterways, Dawson Creek, Prince Rupert, and Vancouver. And they did not flash past, but stopped and even drank; locomotives, emblazoned with the gold crowns which meant they were of the type which had pulled the King and Queen, snorted arrogantly across our path.

As we drove toward Lake Manitoba and I looked back toward Portage, a Ukrainian church with its three bulbous towers, brightly colored, lent the town a romantic flavor; the tall elevators gave it imposing stature. I thought of "Mr. Trow, M.P." who wrote of Portage la Prairie in 1877, when it had a population of three hundred and a grist mill at either end of town, "This is a flourishing village but is at present much the shape of an ant; it requires filling in the centre." I wished that he could see it now. I felt a warm glow of pride in Portage.

All our friends were at Delta, and more had joined the colony. Bob Smith and the Hawkins family, of the Fish and Wildlife Service, had their headquarters here while they made a summer survey of the waterfowl breeding grounds; and Bill Carrick, of Toronto, was making photographic studies of the marsh birds—stunning ones. Bob had a light aircraft parked near by in a cow pasture, and every clear day he disappeared over the horizon. Across the far marshes he went, flying as freely as the waterfowl he was inspecting.

The newcomers were as enthusiastic over their work as the Delta staff, and the spirited discussions we had always held over evening coffee continued. But there was a depressed note in them now, for the local breeding population of wildfowl had taken a sharp drop from the previous year and there were even fewer ducks than there had been in 1938 when the waterfowl were beginning their climb up from the last slump.

Both Bob Smith by plane and Arthur Hawkins in his car, as they traveled far and wide, had noted similar scarcity in breeding ducks, even on areas where food, water, and cover were excellent. Their greatest concern was for the redhead.

"This species never did make a real comeback here," Al said. "It nests late and it's not a very good parent anyway. Many of the young do not take wing until after the gunning season opens, and the new-flying ducklings are shot in great numbers right here on their breeding grounds."

We found the earnest discussions of the group immensely stimulating. "It's the integrity of purpose," Lee said, "that makes places like this the hope of the world."

Now the marsh was not golden, but green and blue. The high grasses billowed in the wind like rough seas, while only tiny furrows dented the azure bays. The ridge road ran like a tunnel through tropical foliage abounding in multitudes of mosquitoes and leaf patterns, choke-cherries dangled in green clusters, and wild roses were heaped high. Wrens, thrushes, and warblers fluttered and sang and squeaked about these bowers; bobolinks bounded in the meadows.

Bob Smith took first me and then Lee up in his two-seated plane to view the marsh from the air. It was exciting to see in one glance the whole region we had explored, and to recognize what an accurate count of birds could be made from a plane.

There were many more ducks than in the spring, for the prairie sloughs were dry now and all the waterfowl of the region had come into the marsh. The males had come to molt and some of them had shed so many wing feathers they were unable to fly. Al had written of seeing drakes fly up and lose such quantities of feathers while they were in the air that they dropped with a flap, and I thought how entertaining it would be to see that from the plane. But all the ducks that were flying kept strictly inside their plumage.

In one large bay there were many hundreds of the big western grebes. We had looked for them vainly in the spring; now from the air their necks looked like pale stems rising from the water, swimming as they were with their bodies submerged. Bob said, through the plane's telephone, that the birds had been breaking out into their courtship dances whenever the plane had flown above them, and it had been quite a sight; lately, however, they had stopped performing and were nesting. "Oh, I can't *bear* to have missed that dance," I shouted loudly above the noise of the motor.

We flew above St. Ambrose too, the Indian settlement in the eastern marsh. We had wanted to drive there, on our former visit, but the lane to it had been impassable. Now we were not dependent on man-made roads, and we soared high above it to gaze on the small houses roofed with straw, the plain little wooden church, the tiny graveyard with its unpainted picket fence. Old trails leading to it across the plain, even abandoned trails, were distinct from the air, so that we looked down on history.

On the ground again, we went in to see the hatchery. It was full of eggs and ducklings looking very spry. Peter was not; he was quite haggard from acting as midwife and nursemaid, to say nothing of cook, waitress, and janitor, for he had to keep a constant heat going, all day and night, in the incubators. He was trying to hatch a pelican egg, and I waited before it, hoping it would begin to peep or cheep aloud as I have heard eggs do before they crack; but it remained stubbornly glum and cryptic.

Peter was studying the young coots, who were peculiar but hardly alluring. A blackish down tipped with red and orange was scattered sparsely over their livid skins, their faces had a belligerent air, owing to the blunt orange bill tipped with blood-red, and they all looked as if they were wearing their mothers' feet.

The ducklings, on the other hand, were enchanting scraps of fluff, varying in color from black to a pale cream. The redhead and canvasback chicks when they first hatched looked exactly alike, mottled buff and brown, but in a short time it was easy to distinguish between them, for the redhead ducklings had round heads like their parents, while the canvasback chicks had the characteristic profile, pointed and severe, of the adults.

We spent Midsummer Day in the canoe—I can't imagine a more perfect way of celebrating it. It was dreamy, delightful weather, and between depths of blue sky and blue water, the slim bulrushes raised decorative heads. How strangely different this landscape was from the massive strength of the Rockies! Water and land seemed a shimmering gauze, a trifle less ethereal than the sky. There was no way of gauging distance at all; the stands of cattails looked like imaginary plateaus, and sleepy pelicans seemed like phantom ships in a distant harbor. Long horizontal ripples ran toward us through the bulrushes.

Some of the pelicans still had the gold discs standing on their yellow bills. They were absurd and solemn on the water, not beautiful as they are in flight. When they fed, they raised their wings as their heads disappeared under the surface. They kicked with both feet at once when rising from the bay, instead of running along as the wild swans had, and when they flew they flapped and then scaled along, their set wings slightly raised above horizontal, their bellies near the water. These birds were nesting on Lake Manitoba and sometimes flew as far as fifty miles to carry food to their young.

As we watched them, some of them began to perform a strange drill. They swam back and forth as if they were marching, all turning at once at an inaudible command. Two separate bands combined and broke up into a social gathering, though they kept giving muffled groans which sounded far from festive. After a time they separated and went back to their patroling again.

Lee once saw an even stranger performance, on Traverse Lake in western Minnesota. With the uncanny bad luck photographers often have, two friends who were taking moving pictures were not with Lee at the moment, to witness the sight which would have convulsed a movie audience.

Thirty pelicans came swimming down a channel, in a tight-packed wedge. They swam leisurely, and now and then the pelicans on the outer edge of the raft would solemnly lower their long bills into the water, all at the same instant. It seemed a ceremonial gesture. There was no hurry, no excitement. No pelican made a hasty second dip, and no bill ever came up with a fish. The ritualistic movement was re-

peated over and over as the wedge zigzagged down the channel, first on one tack and then on the other.

Though the ones in the center were wedged in too tightly to dip their bills, the whole company were so occupied that they were almost upon Lee when one old fellow spied him and flapped up the channel in alarm. The others, however, did nothing so undignified. They merely broke ranks and made their way back upstream, preening themselves unconcernedly as they went.

Not content with our long day in the canoe, we were out again with Pete in the evening. From Windy Landing, the whole zenith turned to a fantastic carnation-pink, while the water was dark with a rosy over-lay. One's heart quivered under this beauty.

It was a hushed evening; the bitterns were quiet now, and only the coots and their young were calling in the reeds. Under light swirls of peach-gold cloud, twenty canvasback drakes came by, with their re-flections making black scrawls in the vivid water. Down an inlet, scaup babies were very active, leaping clear of the surface in the impetus of their dives, and four broods of canvasback ducklings seemed to stay under water most of the time, so that we could see only twinkles of them.

Young coots were about, crazy and grotesque as golliwoggs, and as one went squeaking through the reeds. Pete caught it and set it down in the bottom of the canoe. Its purple head was naked except for red-dish little sideburns, scarlet-and-yellow down stuck out on its black sides. It ran up and down the canoe on its huge splay feet, giving despairing cries. It was an object you would think no one but its mother could love, but Peter regarded it with fond pride and took it home.

And now we had a chance to watch the western grebe close at hand. This striking bird is sometimes called the swan grebe, because of the long snowy neck with a black stripe up the back. Its back is brown, but it often sinks so low in the water that you see only a slim neck traveling along, supporting the black and white head with sparkling ruby eyes. This grebe looks as if it wore a flat black beret, and the

slanting line of it gives a devil-may-care expression to the head; the bright crimson eye and the golden bill add to the dashing effect.

Pete shoved our canoe into the cattails at a narrow neck between two bays, where flotillas of the grebes sailed before us into the farther one. We had disturbed them, and they kept up a high trilling, like tree toads.

Suddenly Lee nudged me with his paddle. "Look out," he muttered fiercely. Over by a patch of grass two grebes were circling. They were

going to dance. We were actually going to have a chance to see that curious activity.

I have always liked grebes because their courtship does not consist in the male showing off before the female; it is a duet-dance on the water, in which both birds take a joyous part. Now one grebe presented a bit of green weed to the other—this is part of the courtship ceremony. Back and forth they swam together, side by side, their movements exactly matched. Then they stood straight up on the water, bowing to right and left, in perfect unison. I could hardly believe we were seeing this, for Bob had said it was almost hopeless to look for it, since the nesting and even the hatching was already in progress.

After bowing, they settled back on the water, but in a minute they were up on the tips of their tails again, and bowing graciously about them. Suddenly they skimmed off over the water together, standing upright as penguins do on land, but moving as swift as speedboats, turning first this way and then that, performing with as perfect rhythm as if one were the mirrored reflection of the other.

Other grebes floated near us, but they hesitated to come through the inlet past our canoe. We finally paddled off, along the edge of tall canes, where we found the grebe nests, platforms of broken bulrushes, each with three or four eggs. Pete said these eggs were heavy when they were newly laid, but floated when they were nearly ready to crack.

Some mothers had already hatched their broods, and now they fled before us with their babies on their backs. Sometimes they dove, with the chicks still couched in their feathers.

One unfortunate child lost his footing and slid off the mother's back as she went down. We paddled over as he swam pluckily along, and I put my hand carefully under the youngster and lifted him up. He was newly hatched and like a very lively powder puff of silver gray. His body was fluffy, his head of pale-gray plush, and a bright little orange star shone on his forehead. "The prettiest thing in the marsh," Pete called him.

He was such a fragile little being that I didn't like to float away with him, far from his mother. I set the chick on the water again, and he began to paddle along beside us, using his tiny black wings like flippers.

As we left the bay I could see that inch of thistledown still floating along, undismayed. I felt as if we had discarded an infant mariner, alone on a wide, wide sea. Pete said the mother would come back for him, and in any case these grebes are self-sufficient from the time they hatch. But he did look far too small to be out by himself at night.

I was delighted beyond measure to find my ruddies still about, and unchanged. Other ducks were far into middle life now—mothers occupied with household cares, fathers losing their fine feathers—but the ruddy was still the gay cavalier of yore, with no family as yet to weight him down. One was napping in the bulrushes, and as he woke he immediately began puffing and chuckling away, his blue bill as dazzling as ever.

I had a feeling of mingled ecstasy and peace, as we floated on the dim water under the last of the bright clouds and the first of the blue dusk. I must state that I am as firm a believer in an actual heaven and hell as any of my forefathers; I differ only in believing that we do not wait for an afterlife to experience them, and I am sure that when we are suffering physical, mental, or moral pangs, if we would only say, "Now I'm in hell; *what* a view!" it would help us to weather the catastrophe. So now, here was heaven for me, and luckily I knew it at the time; and that ruddy and I were afloat in it, rather rudimentary angels.

Lee and I drove away from Delta on a sunny morning. This was the end of our holidaying. Though it had been far more than a holiday, I thought. As we sped along through the bright sunlight I went over all that we had gained.

First an acquaintanceship with Canadian people. Usually only superficial contacts, to be sure, just a few moments' conversation in a hotel or at a filling station. But we had enjoyed these meetings, and we had received a strong impression of honesty and friendliness. We had never been exploited, and over and over, through our trip of ten thousand miles, we had met a pleasant concern at our being so far from home. And though we had sometimes stayed in odd places we had invariably found good beds and adequate food; one thing about such a young country is that if there are any hotels at all they are likely to be fresh new ones.

Our real encounters, of course, had been the ones with wildlife. This had been an intimate, direct communication. Friendships had been made; such varied ones—the mad delight in the ruddy, respectful admiration of the elk, a profound regard for mountain sheep, compassion for the baby moose, to give a few examples. We would remember these all our lives. And these new experiences had multiplied, rather than

213

added to, the wealth of former ones, as the sandhill cranes had increased the value of our ibis adventure manyfold, and the flight of the godwits had enhanced our memory of the soaring cranes.

These meetings are treasured especially, since it seems more difficult for modern man, as he is chipped into more and more intellectual and emotional facets, to come close to his fellows. Even with beloved friends we now find ourselves in contact only at odd points, whereas in simpler times the faith, political belief, and culture of each man often fitted tightly with those of his companions. We may be lonely in a profounder way than man has ever been, all the more because our sympathy and our terror have an ever-widening range.

But we are not so separated from natural things, I thought, looking with gratitude at the tall ferns along the roadside. By some glorious chance, modern men are not barred from mother earth by the intricacies of their spirits. We still come to her in sure understanding, wordless, actual, and durable.

I do not mean by this that our human relationships are not of supreme importance. Nothing is more valuable. But they are intrinsically complicated, and the very fact that they are so precious makes us feel tension, whether or not we realize it. The joy, the challenge, the demands in personal contact, however slight the bond or however dear the fellowship, use up our reserves of sensitivity; the need for understanding and the difficulty of its full achievement calls for infinite and subtle adaptation.

Whereas our contacts with nature are of the utmost simplicity. We do not need to be our best selves, or our worst selves—or indeed any selves at all. One's mood does not affect the happiness of a jackpine or a rock rabbit.

Therefore our friendships with other species refresh us, so that we return to our own ilk with renewed vitality and fortitude—

"Stop! Stop!" I called loudly, interrupting my reverie and making myself jump as well as Lee. *"Wild strawberries!"*

214

I was out of the car before Lee came to a stop. Wild strawberries! The tiny scarlet cones were shining all through the short grass. I felt a surge of triumph. For the last two months I had gazed everlastingly at the pretty white blossoms, wishing they'd grow up. At first I was fond of them, but I am far fonder of the berries, and I had come to feel glints of impatience at the innocent petal faces.

The flavor of these small berries when they are truly ripe is incomparable; there is nothing in the world like their wild, tantalizing sweetness. And each tiny berry has a taste all its own, a tang differing from any other, so that one's interest in them never flags. Besides, I have eaten wild strawberries in such memorable places: in the shade of olive trees at Fiesole, at a sidewalk cafe near Notre Dame, on sunset walks through an Illinois countryside, in a boat on the Thames, along the wild north shore of Lake Superior. . . .

One of the few things I do not understand about Lee is that he does not get excited over wild berries, any more than he does over wildflowers; he will eat them (the former, I mean) if I bring them to him, but he does not pick them. The urge to gather berries must be left over from primeval times, but it seems to be a feminine instinct.

Now Lee got out maps while I wandered along the road, my fingers more and more stained and my bliss increasing. I began to pick the sprays of scarlet berries drooping from green stems—they were as beautiful as holly sprays and far more appetizing. Let me see, I said to myself, sitting down in tall grass where the multitudinous gems incarnadine were bright, what was I thinking about? Oh, yes—friendships with other species than our own.

Those friendships were treasured. But I had known such treasured meetings before. What had been a wholly new experience, on this long journey of ours, was the strong feeling I had discovered for the earth itself. I had been accustomed to take the solid ball beneath us more or less for granted, as we enjoyed the phenomena we found upon it.

But now we had seen its bare and noble face unhidden by man-made veils. After knowing flat immensities, gigantic upheavals, and mighty river courses running down the curve of the globe to three great oceans, I was aware of the basic structure beneath us as I had never been before. Our planet, as such, was actual to me; there was a new significance in the fact that we were on a satellite of the sun. Though that information was not news, being informed about a thing is entirely different from an *experience* of it.

Wonder is about us, and we are so hurried by ephemeral happenings that we forget. I had always been pleased with the fancy that one might adventure from star to star, in future lives, but it had never occurred to me before that I am visiting on one now. I felt a new freedom from that knowledge.

Most important gain of all, however: I knew that I had found a vital affirmation of our own values. If our journey had been a flight, it was a flight not away from, but straight into, reality. Face to face with vast elementals, I had lost "the nervous little clod of wants and ailments which is the self" and found an increased love of life for its own sake. I had wanted nothing at all but our liberty under the sky, the feeling of harmony with the natural forces about us. I had loved this earth of ours as deeply as I was capable of loving it, and I felt content, holding close what I had received in return: a clear assurance of unquenchable life and joy.

Lee honked the horn and stopped to let me in the car. We drove along the road which was darkening into pine woods, sharing the strawberry sprays between us.

Just before we came to the boundary of Canada, a small fawn came out of the shadowy forest and stood looking at us, poised on his tiny hoofs for a long moment before he dashed across the sun-barred road. He was very young, but he was sparkling with life, eager for high adventure, and strong in an assurance of his bright future. In fact, he was a fitting symbol of a Canadian spring.

Date Due

Feb 4
DEC 6 1969

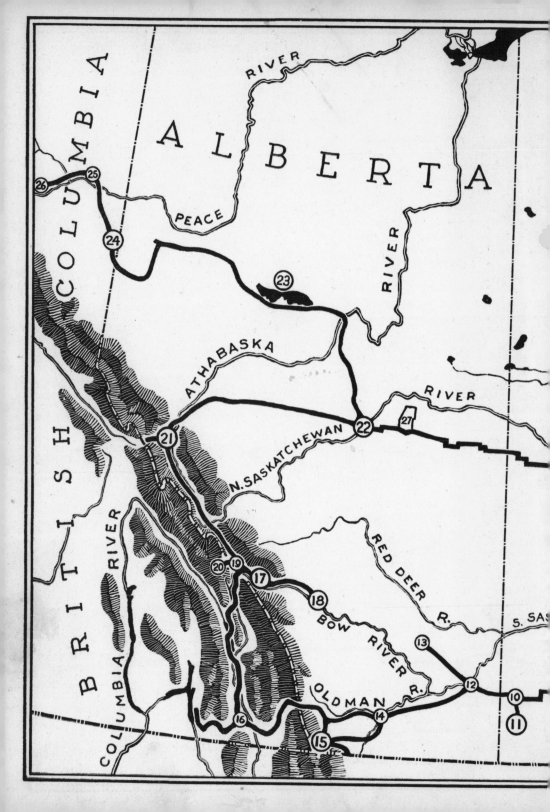